THE
GRIMY
1800s

This book is dedicated to Jimmy Appleby, a Geordie whom I have for many years been proud to call one of my best and most inspiring friends

Other books by André Gren

The Foundation of Brunel's Great Western Railway. (2003) Silver Link Publishing

The Bridge is Down! (2006) Silver Link Publishing

The Victoria Cross: A Chronicle of Courage 1914-1918. (2014)

A Chronicle of Courage: Australian Victoria Cross Winners of the Great War. (2015)

A Chronicle of Courage: The True Stories of Canadian VC Winners of the First World War. (2015)

THE
GRIMY
1800s

WASTE, SEWAGE AND SANITATION
IN NINETEENTH-CENTURY BRITAIN

ANDRÉ GREN

PEN & SWORD
HISTORY

AN IMPRINT OF PEN & SWORD BOOKS LTD.
YORKSHIRE – PHILADELPHIA

First published in Great Britain in 2019 by
PEN AND SWORD HISTORY
An imprint of
Pen & Sword Books Ltd
Yorkshire – Philadelphia

ISBN 978 1 52673 140 1

Printed and bound in the UK by TJ International
Typeset in Times New Roman 11.5/14 by
Aura Technology and Software Services, India

Pen & Sword Books Limited incorporates the imprints of Atlas, Archaeology,
Aviation, Discovery, Family History, Fiction, History, Maritime, Military, Military
Classics, Politics, Select, Transport, True Crime, Air World, Frontline Publishing,
Leo Cooper, Remember When, Seaforth Publishing, The Praetorian Press,
Wharncliffe Local History, Wharncliffe Transport, Wharncliffe True Crime and
White Owl.

For a complete list of Pen & Sword titles please contact
PEN & SWORD BOOKS LIMITED
47 Church Street, Barnsley, South Yorkshire, S70 2AS, England
E-mail: enquiries@pen-and-sword.co.uk
Website: www.pen-and-sword.co.uk

Or

PEN AND SWORD BOOKS
1950 Lawrence Rd, Havertown, PA 19083, USA
E-mail: Uspen-and-sword@casematepublishers.com
Website: www.penandswordbooks.com

Contents

Contents

Acknowledgements

Thanks are due to the Parliamentary Archives, who hold the originals of the documents summarized in this book, and Sally Laurence-Smyth who assisted me greatly in selecting which ones to use. The task of transcribing them, almost all in appalling Victorian manuscript, would have been impossible with my poor vision were it not for the great help I received from Lesley Evans. Our fortnightly sessions were something I looked forward to, both to progress my work and because they were fun. Steve Priestley was always willing and able to help me with all sorts of issues I have had preparing these texts.

The selection of illustrations was eased by assistance from Rav Gopal at Newbury Library, who also gave other essential technical assistance. Jon Wright of Pen and Sword gave me good advice on the format of the book, and a magnificent copy-editing job was carried out by my dear wife, Fiona. Thanks are also due to Will Adams, who did an excellent job of compiling the index of this book.

Thank you all.

André Gren

Introduction

Nineteenth century England and Wales experienced huge changes, thanks mainly to the Industrial Revolution. The population grew from almost 9 million in 1801 to more than 33 million a century later (see Appendix 1), which could be attributed largely to the improvements in public health and the decline of infant mortality. The population would have increased further if it hadn't been for the other demographic phenomenon of the nineteenth century: emigration.

The Industrial Revolution changed the way we worked, which changed the way we lived. Agricultural workers deserted the countryside to work in the cities. Consequently, Britain's large cities showed substantial population increases during the nineteenth century, both in absolute and percentage terms. What was known as the administrative county of London rose from 959,316 in 1801 to 4,536,451 in 1901. In the Midlands, Birmingham's population rose from 84,711 in 1801 to 522,204 in 1901. Elsewhere in the Midlands, Leicester's population grew from 17,005 in 1801 to 65,405 in 1851 and to 211,579 in 1901.

In the north of England, Leeds rose from 53,162 in 1801 to 428,968 in 1901, Liverpool from 77,765 in 1801 to 704,134 in 1901 and Manchester's population grew from 70,409 in 1801 to 543,372 in 1901. The greatest increase in percentage terms was recorded in Bradford, West Yorkshire, which saw a population of 6,000 in 1801 swell to 279,000 in 1901.

The birth rate per thousand fell from forty-one in 1801 to twenty-eight in 1901. However, even though the rate per thousand fell, the absolute number of births grew. According to census office reports, records of births in England and Wales were introduced in 1838, when the figure was 463,787. By 1901, the figure had more than doubled to 929,807. This is because the childbearing population had grown, the number of births had grown and the instances of infant mortality had fallen. The rate of infant mortality per thousand is not available for 1801, but from

1851 to 1901 it fell from 153 to 127 per thousand, thanks in great part to the improvements in public health and sanitation including the increased availability and cleanliness of running water, better sewerage and the introduction of flush toilets.

However, although the population increased quickly in the early nineteenth century, as the century progressed, the rapid increase in urban population, with its associated overcrowding, led to an alarming deterioration in the living conditions of working people. The new manufacturing processes were causing widespread environmental damage. Britain's towns and cities blackened as they were covered with a layer of grime from increasing coal consumption and unabated coal emissions. In 1800, England and Wales used 10 million tons of coal. A century later, as a result of expanding industry and locomotive engines, the figure was 250 million tons.

Consequently, the mid-nineteenth century saw a slowdown (which picked up again in the early twentieth century, when Britain's population rose faster than ever before) but this continued for only as long as it took for new laws to pass that brought in major improvements in public health.

This book does not attempt to offer an authoritative account of the reasons for the growth in Britain's population in the nineteenth century but concentrates instead on the consequences of that growth and the increasing need for what was termed 'nuisance control'.

In the fifteenth century, to cause a 'nuisance' meant to inflict harm or injury, but by the nineteenth century the term was being used to refer to inconvenience and annoyance. The quaint-sounding 'inspectors of nuisances' were appointed with wide-ranging responsibilities. In modern day, these would be environmental health officers and health and safety officers and those employed to deal with antisocial behaviour.

The success of the inspectors of nuisances, who were all over England and Wales, can be seen in the increased life expectancy at birth throughout the nineteenth century. In 1801 in England and Wales, men and women were only expected to live to 40. By 1901, men had a life expectancy of 45 and women of 49. This increase is not entirely due to the work of nuisance inspectors, but their contribution, which is mapped out in this book, is certainly substantial.

The Municipal Corporations Act of 1835 reformed local government and granted corporations new powers through a succession of private bills, which were brought forward under the Nuisances Removal Act of 1846. Inspectors of nuisances all over Britain would argue for or against the bill during an evidence session in front of a select committee.

Inspectors covered a range of nuisances that threatened public health. Many concerned the supply and cleanliness of running water. As late as 1907, Saddleworth's inspector of nuisances, John Bradbury, reported that people had to put off their washing day because the water was running dirty.

Other examples include Frank White, inspector of nuisances in Bradford, noting that an ice-cream seller kept his stock in pots covered by the same blankets he used for his horses, which were often smeared with horse dung. In London, inspector Alfred Taylor reported bodies floating out of the graves buried 3 or 4 foot (ft) deep in unsuitable non-porous clay. He warned that this was encouraging the 'disgusting' practice of burning the remains of the dead. In 1908, William Tyldesley, Leicester's inspector of nuisances, reported that he had found a number of emaciated beasts ready for sale at butchers' shops in the town and meat that was unfit for human consumption. James Brown, the inspector of nuisances at Mynyddislwyn in Wales, informed the committee that filthy rag-and-bone men were distributing sweets to children while they were collecting the town's night soil (human faeces).

Most of the evidence sessions were summarized and recorded immediately after the session and these, mostly manuscript summaries, are available in the Parliamentary Archives in the House of Lords. This book presents edited summaries of the most interesting evidence sessions. The sessions are organized around themes of different types of nuisances. Figures are given for the population in 1801, 1851 and 1901 of each location featured.

This series of snapshots from Britain, which was struggling to cope with rampant population growth and rapid urbanization reminds us of how hard-won these advances in sanitation were – advances that today we take for granted.

Chapter 1

Nuisance Control and Removal in Nineteenth-Century Britain

The population of Britain grew almost fourfold during the nineteenth century and turned villages into urban areas and towns into cities. All this took place when there was hardly any running water, hardly any sewage disposal systems and hardly any flush toilets. The misery of living in such poor sanitary conditions was commented on by the great social commentator of the day, Charles Dickens. In 1864, Dickens wrote in his weekly magazine *Household Words* that 'the preventable wretchedness and misery in which the mass of the people dwell, the reform of their habitations must precede all other reforms.... . Without it, all other reforms must fail.'

Large areas of cities simply stank, and this didn't go unnoticed by Dickens either. In his novel, *Dombey and Son,* published in monthly parts between 1846 and 1848, he called on his readers to 'look round upon the world of odious sights...breathe the polluted air, foul with every impurity that is poisonous to health and life.'

This striking aside, written in October or November 1847, probably owed a good deal of its urgency to the recent threat of a cholera outbreak. A series of letters published in *The Times* and elsewhere noted the alarming reappearance of cholera in Eastern Europe and its likely return to England. But if a newly heightened consciousness of epidemic disease lay behind this passage – deliberate propaganda for the public health and sanitary cause – it also owed much to Dickens' interest in sanitary and public health reform and his habit of making outspoken comments about the absence of regulation on sanitary conditions.

He ranted against what he described as 'state inaction' during the cholera epidemic at the end of the 1840s, railing against culpable negligence (again at the national level) that was repeated during the 1853-54 epidemic, which Dickens likened to wholesale murder. In his preface to an 1849 edition of *Martin Chuzzlewit*, Dickens wrote: 'In all my writings I have taken every available opportunity of showing the want of sanitary improvements in the neglected dwellings of the poor.'

Disposing of human waste has always been a problem in Britain. The Romans used garderobe shafts (a hole in the floor leading to a cesspit or moat), as did the Normans in their castles. Subsequent generations sought other solutions. For the Tudors, there were three types of toilet, depending on status at court. Henry VIII had a padded seat (sometimes stuffed with swansdown and covered with velvet) over a chamber pot. Lower down the social order, there were personal ceramic chamber pots and communal facilities (called houses of easement). Medieval London had a number of such systems, including an eighty-four-seater, which washed out into the Thames. Garderobes, padded stools, earth closets (using dry earth to cover the waste) middens (refuse heaps), Whittington's Longhouse (a public toilet in Cheapside with 128 seats and named after London's Lord Mayor, Richard Whittington with whose money it was built), cesspits and chamber pots all emptied into the street; none provided an ideal solution to the disposal of human waste.

By the early nineteenth century, London had a population of almost one million and over 200,000 cesspits, and public health had become a serious problem. The first cholera outbreak occurred in 1831. In all there were five such outbreaks, culminating in the Great Stink of 1858, when London was overwhelmed by pungent and noxious smells.

By the mid-1800s, the new local government bodies established under the Municipal Corporations Act of 1835 were beginning to take responsibility for the health hazards caused by poor sanitation. As the new corporations struggled to cope with their expanding populations, they asked Parliament to grant them new powers through a succession of private bills, which were brought forward under the Nuisances Removal Act of 1846.

One area in which the new local government bodies flexed their muscles was in superintending the introduction of running water and flush toilets.

The bills were there to allow the newly created local authorities to deal with a range of nuisances, from disposal of 'night soil', which was collected regularly by scavengers, who would load their carts with the filth from each home and take it off to the nearest river and throw it into the water; to the provision of fresh running water; to coping with the new phenomenon of unruly seaside cyclists. In London, there were concerns about drinking water being polluted by human remains buried in graves cut into the shallow, non-porous clay on which much of the city had been built. Elsewhere, concerns were expressed about how much people must pay for the supply of drinking water through the innovation of taps in domestic homes.

The first 'inspector of nuisances' was Thomas Fresh who was appointed as the inspector for Liverpool in 1844. Inspectors sprung up all over England and Wales and they would bring up issues that affected their residents to evidence sessions in front of select committees. There were 208,375 such sessions in the nineteenth century. The total number of sessions relating to nuisance bills was 345 over about seventy years.

In 1846, the Nuisances Removal and Diseases Prevention Act was passed to help improve sanitation in order to stem the spread of cholera. Of the 345 nuisance evidence sessions held following the passing of the Act to its repeal in 1915, 218 feature men who describe their profession as inspector of nuisances.

In 1856, the London-wide Metropolitan Board of Works (the precursor to London City Council) was established. Its aim was to provide the infrastructure to cope with the capital's growth and one of its major achievements was the creation of the London sewerage system, started by the board's chief engineer, Joseph Bazalgette, in 1859. It would not be completed until 1875, despite the Prince of Wales officially opening it in 1865.

Inspectors of nuisances came across as often overworked and sometimes overwhelmed, with some less than qualified to hold their posts and others not so diligent. In 1861, Birmingham's inspector of nuisances, James Bliss, explained to a committee his impressively diverse range of responsibilities, which included overcrowded courts, dwelling houses, ash pits (dry water closets), lodging houses, slaughterhouses and hackney carriages.

An inspector would often be appointed when an area became blighted with a problem but they were not paid handsomely for their work. Thomas Rees from Guildford told his select committee in 1886 that he did not know if he would be able to carry on with his duties on his salary of £130 a year, were it not for his wife having private means. This salary equates to just over £10,000 a year today. Not a lot for a full-time job in Surrey.

However, changes didn't happen overnight and not all solutions were perfect, or even fit for purpose. Many inspectors reported that, despite the supply of running water and the installation of toilets, many people continued to live in filthy, unsanitary conditions with groups fighting over single public taps from which only a trickle would appear. And these 'improvements' did little for the environment. It was not uncommon for private homes and factories to empty their waste and sewage directly into brooks, dykes, streams and rivers.

No water closet, no problem. In 1896, James Franklin, the inspector of nuisances for Finchley in London, told his committee that people merely stood at the entrance of bars and urinated there, and the urine flowed across the footway.

However, not every inspector was too bothered about sanitation. In 1881, John Vickers, Beverley's inspector of nuisances, reassured his select committee that people were not nearly as dirty as they had been described.

In terms of sanitation, two of the biggest life-changing achievements in the nineteenth century were the supply of running water and the introduction of the flushing toilet. Yet not even the wealthy could take these advancements for granted and some of Britain's great houses didn't have running water installed until relatively late. While the Charles Barry-designed Highclere Castle in Berkshire (the setting of Downton Abbey) included running water when it was built in 1863, Blenheim Palace in Oxfordshire didn't install flushing toilets until the 1880s, and bathrooms with baths and running water were not fitted until 1934. At Cragside in Northumberland, built by William Armstrong, flushing toilets were installed in 1872, but were not followed by hot and cold running water until later in the century. At Castle Howard in North Yorkshire, flushing toilets were recommended in a report of 1882, which was acted upon shortly afterwards.

However, Chatsworth House, home to the Duke and Duchess of Devonshire, had running water from at least the 1st Duke's time (1684-1700), located in what was then known as the Stag's Parlour, and the bath ran hot and cold water. Several flushing toilets were installed in 1706: the pots of these were normally of alabaster, and the woodwork of cedar or oak. The brasswork, bought at auction in 1706, one must suppose would have been connected with the flushing mechanism. Interestingly, after the 1st Duke's time, sanitary provision ceased to be

4

of concern and at least ten of his toilets were removed. It was not until the 9th Duke's succession in 1908 that plumbing at Chatsworth reached modern standards.

Flushing toilets have been credited to Thomas Crapper, an engineer born in Yorkshire in 1836. In 1861, he started his own business manufacturing sanitaryware, bathroom fittings and the flush toilet, which became regular household items and made the firm famous. Some 'Crapper' manhole covers may still be seen in Westminster Abbey today. The firm attracted the attention of the royal family and Crapper was commissioned to fit the royal country house of Sandringham with thirty water closets, all with cedar wood seats. The company obtained several royal warrants.

However, as the 1706 installation of flushing toilets in Chatsworth House proves, it wasn't his invention. The device was actually created by Sir John Harington, a courtier of Elizabeth I, who had a 'john' (a slang term still used in the United States today) built at Richmond Palace. It was developed by Alexander Cummins, whose device allowed a modicum of water to remain in the bowl to prevent seepage from the sewers. However, Crapper did popularize the flush toilet and made it an accepted domestic fixture.

The notion that Crapper gave his scatological name to faeces is also, disappointingly, not correct. The word 'crap', according to the *Oxford English Dictionary*, derives from the Middle English 'crappe', meaning chaff or residue from rendered fat.

In the following pages, each evidence session is prefaced by the title of the bill being presented to the committee. This gives the reader an idea of what the promoters of the bill were seeking. There is also a table of the village, town or city's population growth, which contains the data for 1801 (the first census), 1851 and 1901. These tables demonstrate the surge in population that occurred all over England and Wales in the nineteenth century.

Chapter 2

Overcrowding:
Living Conditions and Privies

Bradford 1850, John Gordon

> *He had found many of the lodging houses in an exceedingly*
> *improper, unclean and miserable condition; many were*
> *nurseries of crime and disease.*

Bill for repealing an Act relating to the Borough of Bradford in the
County of York and for better paving, lighting, watching, draining and
otherwise improving the said Borough, and for the better regulation and
management thereof.

Bradford population growth

1801	6,000
1851	108,000
1901	279,000

John Gordon was the officer in charge of the removal of nuisances in
Bradford, West Yorkshire, and gave evidence to Parliament in 1850.
A surgeon, he had been living in Bradford for nearly nineteen years. He
was a member of the Nuisance Removal Committee, which was appointed
to carry out the Nuisances Removal and Diseases Prevention Act of 1846.

His duty was to call upon, inspect and report upon nuisances but, to
his dismay, he found the process for their abatement was lengthy and
delayed. It was a matter of painful regret to Gordon that when he had to
deal with nuisances of a most serious character, he didn't have the power
to do anything for a month. He supported the proposed bill as he thought
it would remedy these defects.

Overcrowding: Living Conditions and Privies

In the summer and autumn of 1849, Bradford suffered a severe outbreak of cholera and more than 200 cases were brought to Gordon's notice. The disease had broken out in a district called New Leeds and the committee members were directed to ascertain, if possible, the cause. On inspection, they found several streets in which there was not a single drain, and their attention was directed to a privy immediately under a house from which a corpse had been removed a short time before.

The privy was open and extended to a number of houses on each side. The stench was so offensive, the members were compelled to leave immediately, which they did but not before searching the house and finding a child in an advanced stage of cholera.

Gordon felt that, considering the circumstances, he should have the power to enforce the construction of proper conveniences. He felt it was privies like these, situated underneath filthy, crowded houses that were to blame for the spread of cholera in his area.

Four years earlier, Gordon had been directed to lodging houses in Bradford, such as the ones on Lower West Street where none of the twenty-seven houses was fit for human habitation but each was home to at least ten people. He had visited similar dwellings, along with a local clergyman, with a view to effecting an improvement in the condition of the female factory operatives, a great many of whom lived in such houses. He had found many of the lodging houses in an exceedingly improper, unclean and miserable condition; many were nurseries of crime and disease.

Although he was powerless to enforce change, he thought the town council should support the bill that no person should be allowed to let a property as a lodging house that was not rated up to £10. Gordon thought such a provision was calculated in a way to elevate the respectability of the lodging house as well as those occupying them and would help prevent disease and crime.

He wasn't alone in his opinions. He'd had conversations with many medical associates in Bradford and all agreed that the town was deficient in aspects of public hygiene. In fact, not one medical man had signed a petition against the bill and Gordon believed that no one in the town was opposed to it. It was felt necessary for the preservation of the health of the residents that the council should be armed with further powers, and that it would be dangerous to delay the measure any longer.

Birmingham 1861, James Bliss

*He found it was the entire sewage that had drained from three
or four nearby streets, which housed around 1,000 people
and in which dead dogs were floating.*

Bill for transferring to the Mayor, Aldermen and Burgesses of the
said Borough the estates, properties and effects now vested in certain
Commissioners having jurisdiction over parts of the Borough and to
provide for the better draining, lighting, paving, supplying with water
and otherwise improving the said Borough and making provision for
the good government, regulation and management thereof and for the
regulation and simplification of the system of rating therein.

Birmingham population growth

1801	84,711
1851	232,538
1901	522,204

In 1861, Birmingham's inspector of police, James Bliss, gave evidence
in the House of Lords on the Birmingham Improvement Bill. He told
the committee he had also been appointed by the Watch Committee as
inspector of nuisances. He was well-acquainted with the borough and,
since his appointment, had removed a great many nuisances.

Despite his good work, Bliss said the borough still had issues that
were dangerous to the health of the residents, but as these fell outside
the boundaries of the Nuisances Removal Act, he thought they
required some special enactment to get rid of them. He acknowledged
that some of them had been removed by volunteers who felt so
endangered and annoyed that they had decided to do something about
it themselves.

His evidence applied in particular to the hamlets of Duddeston and
Nechells where, generally speaking, the houses were of a poorer character.
They were small lodging houses, which Bliss described as 'lower-rented
houses'. The residents had complained to him on numerous occasions.

His findings were as follows: on Richard Street the entire sewage
from the courts ran onto the waste ground at the back, which was mixed
with the filth and privies, and remained stagnant – a complete bog.

Lord Street was in a similar condition. The sewage ran on the surfaces, and in some instances through the privies, finding its level where it could and lying a foot deep in places.

In Coleman Street, the courts drained into cesspools, or whatever one might choose to call them. Again, the filth was about a foot deep. The privy ran into it and was full of pots and kettles and all kinds of household equipment.

Bliss regretted that there was no power under the existing board to remedy those nuisances and nor did he have the power to remove them. If he did get a place cleared, it would be as bad again in a week, and some people complained that removing the nuisances in that way did as much damage as just leaving them alone.

Bliss told the committee that about a fortnight before, he had received complaints about water under the railway arches. He sent an officer to examine it and he found it was the entire sewage that had drained from three or four nearby streets, which housed around 1,000 people and in which dead dogs were floating. He contacted the railway company because he thought they might remove it. They responded to say they were willing to have the hollows filled but, if they did, the nuisance would be worse than before. The filth could not be removed unless a proper drain was made. But whose duty it was to provide the drains, Bliss did not know. He was unaware of any power to make proper drains and if such power did exist, it had certainly not been exercised.

Bliss advised the committee that it was not his business to argue over who was responsible for these nuisances, that fell outside the jurisdiction of the Act, he simply wanted them removed.

Rotherham 1863, John Jennings

The residents were predominantly the lowest class of large Irish families. There would be the father, mother and perhaps a son or daughter and husband, and some six or eight children.

Bill for enabling the Local Board of Health for the district of Rotherham and Kimberworth in the West Riding of the County of York to construct and maintain an improved system of waterworks, for the supply of the district and adjacent places with water, and for enabling the Board to purchase the existing markets and fairs within the district and to establish new markets and fairs within the district, and to purchase and extinguish dues and duties paid and collected within the town of Rotherham and for amending Acts relating to the District and for other purposes.

Rotherham population growth
1801	17,191
1851	31,386
1901	119,815

John Jennings had held the position of inspector of nuisances in Rotherham, South Yorkshire for more than ten years when he appeared before the committee concerned with the Rotherham and Kimberworth Local Board of Health Bill.

Rotherham's water supply came from springs and Jennings had discovered that the supply of water for domestic, sanitary and other purposes was insufficient for the town's inhabitants. In summer and autumn, they only had water for two to four hours of a twenty-four hour day. Jennings recalled a cholera epidemic in the autumn of the previous year. At that time, the water supply was limited and everyone – he and residents alike – were of the opinion that the district had suffered greatly because of it.

He told the committee that during an epidemic one July, he inspected a locality called Orchard Masbrough, along with a local doctor. On arrival, they were surrounded by people who begged the doctor to give them more water. They had tried the tap – this was about 11am – and there was no water. This tap had to supply about thirty houses in which there were about 140 inhabitants. They explained that they would usually be without water from 11am until 7am the following morning.

Jennings said the families had no means of storing the water and described the cholera epidemic in that quarter as 'very fatal', which he attributed principally to the lack of water. Jennings explained that while this was just one example, he was confident it was the same in all the cottage houses in his district as they suffered from overcrowding. Ordinarily, the small cottages contained two rooms, one above and one below, and they were built back-to-back, with a small yard but no means of ventilation. The residents were predominantly the lowest class of large Irish families. There would be the father, mother and perhaps a son, or daughter and husband, and some six or eight children.

Jennings believed the limited water supply also meant it was impossible to remove nuisances, and he had reported this to the board several times in the past few years. The number of privies, specifically ash pits, in which waste was simply covered by soil, was rising. Ash pits were not supposed to accumulate and yet, due to the cramped conditions, most people had one no more than 2 or 3ft from their front door or window. The filth and stench were intolerable.

As the ash pits couldn't be moved further away, Jennings proposed that they be replaced with water closets. He had even gone so far as to trial the replacement of ash pits with water closets in some instances, but on inspecting them had found that due to the lack of regular water, these had also become a nuisance.

It was the custom of the cottagers to use the solid contents of their privies as fertilizer for farming. Liquid matter, meanwhile, was running into Whiston Brook. The entire village of Whiston also drained into the brook, which meant the water was certainly not fit to drink, or suitable for domestic purposes.

Several springs also ran into the brook and in Jennings' judgment, 20,000 gallons were being discharged every twenty-four hours. He wanted to see a way of securing this pure spring water before it ran into the brook and became contaminated, as this would benefit the residents immeasurably. The clean water was there, the waterworks system just needed to be changed so the people could access it.

As well as being inspector for nuisances, Jennings acted for the Board of Health, which had responsibility for the town's markets and in this capacity, he brought up an issue concerning Rotherham Market. He had been aware of the market for some thirty years but times were changing and it was no longer fit for purpose. He calculated that in 1831, the population served by the market in Rotherham, Kimberworth and adjacent villages would have been 10,000 and now it was upwards of 30,000. Jennings thought the market was inadequate for the larger population. The marketplace itself was too small and, on market days, the streets leading to it were filthy and blocked with stalls and vehicles of all descriptions, and there had been many accidents.

An old parliamentary law, dating from 1801, restricted the sale of meat to within the marketplace, which meant there were around twenty butchers' stalls and a large amount of animal products in one small area. Having this exclusivity on meat products kept the price high and Jennings told the committee it drove a great many people to Sheffield, to save perhaps one pence per pound weight. He said that not only would a bigger, less congested marketplace serve the residents better but lifting the restriction on where meat could be sold, would prevent people from heading out of town to buy it.

Bridlington 1893, Henry Jackson

> *Bridlington was plagued with groups of between twelve and twenty people on bicycles and tricycles riding forwards and backwards and racing three or four abreast.*

Bill to vest in the local board for the district of Bridlington certain lands and hereditaments at Bridlington Quay now held in trust for them and to confer on the said local board further powers for the good government of their district and for other purposes.

Bridlington population growth

1801	3,773
1851	6,846
1901	10,023

The following example doesn't link directly to overcrowding but it is an indication of the nuisances created when lots of people lived together in built-up areas. In 1894 a House of Commons committee met to hear evidence from Henry John Jackson on the Bridlington Local Board bill. Jackson was the chairman of the Pleasure Boat Committee in the East Yorkshire coastal town.

Jackson explained that Bridlington was plagued with groups of between twelve and twenty people on bicycles and tricycles riding forwards and backwards and racing three or four abreast. This was a great impediment to pedestrians, especially on the busy esplanade, which attracted people from all parts of town and could at times become crowded.

Jackson was asked whether his complaint would be dealt with if he was given control over the esplanade and sea walls. While he acknowledged that this was where the problem was located and he was keen to stop it, he replied that granting him the power to ban it in that area would only drive the two and three-wheeled nuisances to other parts of town, where they would continue on the asphalted roads in the same fashion.

Jackson wanted his power to be extended to cover the area bounded by King Street, Princes Street and the esplanade and specifically that 'it shall be lawful for the Local Board from time to time by order to prohibit, during such period as may be specified in the order, the use of bicycles on the esplanade and the sea walls now or hereafter to be constructed by the Local Board or the roads or promenades thereon.'

East Ham 1903, Joseph Banks

> *As they had no water supply, they would knock on the door of the nearest house, and if the people there refused to supply them with water they would smash the windows and threaten all kinds of violence.*

Bill to confer further powers upon the Urban District Council for the district of East Ham in the county of Essex.

East Ham population growth

1801	1,165
1855	1,550
1901	96,008

When Joseph Banks, the inspector of nuisances for East Ham in London, faced the committee to talk about the East Ham Improvement Bill in 1903, he described an East Ham that is very different from the congested area it is today. He explained that among the houses there were several large pieces of land, which were occupied by groups of people he described as 'squatters'.

These squatters, who lived in caravans, and travelled the country entertaining the locals, were pitching up in East Ham and staying for a few days or longer and were creating a number of problems. As they had no water supply, they would knock on the door of the nearest house, and if the people there refused to supply them with water they would smash the windows and threaten all kinds of violence. Banks thought this problem could only be solved if the bill prohibited the travellers from coming within 200ft of any dwelling house.

He also claimed their living arrangements were insanitary to the point of being a risk to public health, as they carried infectious diseases that were being spread within the community.

Another major problem was the noise they made, especially when they put on pleasure shows and roundabouts (hand or steam-powered carousels), which he said attracted 'rough and vulgar people'. Banks described the noise as 'hideous', and said local residents were being kept up till 1 or 2am. When asked to recall an incident of a show carrying on into the small hours, he said it occurred frequently, most notably on public holidays such as a recent Easter Monday and every bank holiday. He referred specifically to the Bowling Estate on the Barking Road. He stressed that he didn't have any complaint to make about the showpeople, only the general environment, by which he meant the people who followed the shows as they were badly behaved and a great annoyance to the local residents.

The committee asked Banks to give his most careful consideration to this point, because the owners of the show which appeared on the Bowling Estate had given evidence to say they did not remain open after midnight. Banks said the show he had been referring to was 'here today and gone tomorrow'. The committee said they were referring to the same show and that it had closed before 11pm. Banks reconsidered his accusation and said the show might have closed at midnight, but then the people it brought with it did not go home until the next morning. Banks hoped his bill would curb this practice by preventing them from coming at all.

He spoke of another nuisance caused by their presence. He said at least five or six bookmakers were on the street every day and would take slips of paper and money from women and children as well as the men. Banks knew the names of several of these bookmakers and could tell the committee the very corner in which they would stand and the lamppost they would lean against. He said they carried on their business wherever there were groups of men, especially builders. He said he'd seen half-built houses with bookmakers standing in the middle of hod-carrying tradesmen, who would lay down their threepences and sixpences on a horse.

The committee observed that there was a bye-law in force in East Ham that any person who frequented or used any highway, street or other public place for betting, bookmakering or wagering could be prosecuted. However, Banks observed that the penalty was so small – just £5 – that these bookmakers would come up to court with the penalty in their pocket, put the money down on the clerk's desk and walk out smiling.

Banks said it was impossible to get rid of the travellers. The committee asked why the police didn't act but Banks said the police were powerless as they were pitched on private ground by arrangement of the landlord. If the travellers were on a public highway, the police could move them on. The county council or the police had some powers if the squatters were within a limited distance from a house, but, for the most part, they remained just outside that distance, and even if they did breach that law, the police failed to act and it was left to others to do something.

He said he had never known the police to take the initiative. The committee asked whether Banks ever went to a constable and said, 'I call your attention to this bye-law, and I require you to get these people moved on.' Banks replied that he had done this several times. He had written to the chief officers at Scotland Yard and the heads of different police centres and never, during his nine years, had he known them to move the travellers on.

The committee asked if the county council had a bye-law it could use. Banks said it had, but the police were the administrators of the bye-law. He would inform the police when the travellers came but invariably some days would elapse before any move was made, and generally no move was made whatsoever. The committee asked Banks if he had ever applied to the county council to enforce their bye-law, which penalized the owner of land who permitted it to be used for the annoyance of other persons. Banks said he had not. The committee suggested that he ought to have done that. He agreed, but observed that the owner of the land argued that he was a poor fellow who was in a bad position.

The committee asked Banks about the travellers, who were coming from Kent and the other side of the river and heading to the higher districts of Essex. Banks said he could see no reason why they should stop in East Ham. He pointed out that if they moved a little further north there were large open spaces of land, such as Wanstead Flats and portions of Epping Forest, where these shows were permitted, subject to the regulations of the Corporation of London, and they would make as much money there as they did in East Ham.

If they went even further north or east, they would find themselves in open country, which would be perfect for their shows. But, of course, it would not be so convenient for their chattel-selling in London. The committee asked Banks if it would be any inconvenience or hardship if these people were not permitted to stop in East Ham, and were moved on to the open spaces. Banks thought it would be better for their own health and for the people of East Ham too.

The committee asked Banks if he knew much about West Ham, and he told them he had been inspector of nuisances there for two years. West Ham, he said, was similar in character to East Ham but in West Ham they had the power to make or exercise these bye-laws themselves. Banks had acted under these bye-laws several times. Banks concurred with a suggestion by the committee that it was because of his experience there, that he had thought it ought to apply to East Ham.

The committee asked that, supposing East Ham got this clause, how did Banks propose to effect it? He reiterated that he simply sought power to rid East Ham of these people and their nuisances completely.

Chapter 3

Grime: Wells, Drains and Discharges

Thirsk 1879, John Wright

> *Asked if the people who didn't have wells had to go either to the public pump or beg or borrow or steal from their neighbours, he received the somewhat hard-hearted response that they had to do as they pleased.*

Bill for confirming certain provisional orders made by the board of trade under the Gas and Water Works Facilities Act, 1870, relating to Cleethorpes Gas, Dorchester Gas, Dron Field Gas, Eckington Gas, Enfield Gas, Havant Gas, Longridge Gas, Northfleet Gas, Wantage Gas, Wellingborough Gas, Dorking Water, Herts and Essex Water, Maidstone Water, Margate Water, Mexborough and District Water, Oystermouth Water, Rhyl District Water, Saint Albans Water, Shoreham and District Water, Stourbridge Water, Thirsk District Water, Aldershot Gas and Water, Ventnor Gas and Water and Ystrad Gas and Water.

Thirsk population growth	
1801	3,885
1851	6,792
1901	7,055

John Wright was a builder and inspector of nuisances in Thirsk, North Yorkshire and was the first inspector of the Rural Sanitary Authority appointed under the Public Health Bill of 1872. Having lived in Thirsk for twenty years, he was well-accustomed to the 57 or 58 acres of Thirsk and Sowerby that fell under his responsibility. In 1879 he gave evidence in the House of Commons on the Gas and Water Provisional Order Confirmation (Thirsk District Water) Bill.

Wright had inspected some wells in the towns of Thirsk and Sowerby and reported some to the sanitary authorities as the water was contaminated and not fit for the purposes of washing, let alone drinking. The soil in the area was very porous and meant that, in many cases, sewage got into the wells.

Wright referred to a well in Mr Fawcett's yard in St James's Green that adjoined the burial ground of the Wesleyan Chapel. That well was closed by order of the Rural Sanitary Authority in 1872, due to drainage from the yard getting into the well and contaminating the water. Seven houses depended on that well for their supply and subsequently, all seven had to get their water from elsewhere.

He gave another example where two wells were supplying around twenty-five houses in Sowerby. Wright had to report them for producing water that was totally unfit for human consumption. In this case the drain was altered with an open joint pipe being replaced by a sanitary pipe. Despite the changes, Wright still had doubts as to whether that water was safe. There was a considerable number of ash pits close by and as the subsoil was porous, it was likely that the filtration from that source got into the well. He insisted that further steps be taken and the cesspool was done away with.

In Wright's view, the wells in Thirsk and Sowerby were not able to produce a good and wholesome supply of water. It was also hard water; so hard it was difficult to use even for washing. Often, residents tried to catch rainwater to wash with, rather than use the wells.

Wright had to report on a well in Long Street, which supplied eight cottages. In that case, the water was foul with sewage and liquid from the ash pits. Wright read his report to the committee:

> 'The pump that supplies the whole of these cottages was situated in the yard known as Johnson's Yard, Long Street. The water in it was very bad, and totally unfit to be used for domestic or other purposes. The yard contains two privies and ash pits that were in close proximity to the well, and not made water-tight at the bottom. The consequence was that the liquid from them percolated through the soil and contaminated the water. There was also a grate in the yard that received the whole of the sewage water from cottages. This was near the well, and will also contribute to fouling it.'

He had also gone to Sowerby and found out how many private and public wells there were in relation to the number of houses. There were 382 houses and 129 pumps. However, there was only one public pump and all the rest were private and attached to the houses. When Wright was asked if the people who didn't have wells had to go either to the public pump or beg or borrow or steal from their neighbours, he received the somewhat hard-hearted response that they had to do as they pleased.

Wright told the committee that the Rural Sanitary Authority had no means whatsoever of remedying the defect in the supply except by ordering other wells to be sunk, but those wells would only be liable to the same cause of contamination.

Thus, he said it would be of great benefit to the town if a water company was established to supply it with good, clean water from a distance. He believed that not doing so would damage the local economy. He raised the point that houses fit for well-heeled people were in the process of being built and currently, the only means of supplying those houses was from the dirty wells. Wright pointed out that it would be highly inconvenient to build such a class of home without a proper water supply.

Horfield 1887, Charles White

If you dip into a man's pocket, you begin to touch a very tender place with him.

Bill for incorporating Bristol Consumers Water Company, and empowering them to construct waterworks and supply water, and for other purposes.

Horfield population growth
1801	119
1851	998
1901	6,712

Charles White, the inspector of nuisances at Horfield in Bristol, gave evidence in the House of Lords in 1887 on the Bristol Consumers Water Bill. Before being appointed as inspector in November 1886, he had been working for the local surveyor.

In White's district there were some 1,200 houses. Of these, 241 were supplied with water from wells and one was supplied from rainwater collected in a cistern and condensed. White's impression was that most of the wells were surface wells, which meant they took their water from very close to ground level. However, a large number of the wells had been closed as the water wasn't fit to drink. Indeed, he had been afraid to drink the water supplied to his own house, and had it analyzed at great expense by Mr Parry, the medical officer for the Horfield Local Board.

The committee asked White what steps were taken to result in a well being closed. He said that if he received a complaint about the quality of the water, he would wash out a bottle and fill it with a sample from the well and take it to the medical officer, explaining from which well and at which time he obtained the sample. He would then report to the board and at this point he considered his job done, as the board would then organize getting the sample analyzed.

If the medical officer condemned the water, the board would then compel the owners of the property to put in a service pipe from Bristol Water Company at their own cost and start paying a monthly service charge. White explained that closing a well came with serious problems and referred to a recent case where residents were without water for a considerable time and had to travel long distances just to find some to drink. They would come to White's well, and he would hand them water over his garden wall.

Although he did not know of anyone who preferred to go without water rather than pay for the pipe, many people would avoid laying out the cost if it was at all possible. Asked why, he said the well had cost them nothing while the water company's charge was considered to be excessive. White was the collector of the poor rates (the tax imposed on each property) and people often complained to him personally about the charges.

Very few houses in White's district had a water closet. While he couldn't give the committee exact figures, he said he was recently called upon to examine a privy on a street and he believed it was the only one for the entire street.

The committee wondered how these privies or closets were cleaned in the absence of a good water supply due to the number of shut wells. White said that they weren't: whenever he'd had to examine them they had always been choked. The committee said surely the people using the privies had a responsibility to clean them and White said residents were obliged to flush their privies with buckets of water from their wells but added that this was only done if one of the residents was a clean, decent woman who did not mind the trouble.

The committee observed that the previous witness, (Richard Brown, chairman of Horfield Local Board) had explained that groups of houses were supplied with water from a public tap. White said the distance from tap to house was generally some 100 to 200 yards (yds) and that the class of people living in the houses would not travel that far to obtain water simply to flush out the privy.

The water company would supply water to the privy for a charge of £10 but White thought residents considered this to be prohibitive, especially as they had already paid out for the pipes to be laid. White, himself, had to pay the cost at his own house in Horfield.

Despite these complaints, the people of Horfield were strongly in favour of passing the bill and constructing waterworks. Of that, he said, there was no doubt. He heard this every day from the residents. The committee suspected he had come to this conclusion from casual conversations with friends but White dismissed this. He said people were reading in the newspapers that the Horfield Local Board had agreed to present a petition in favour of the bill, and they were talking about it constantly, and asking officials, like him, what they were going to do.

He added, that, according to what had been written in the newspapers, if the bill was passed, people would get their water under the rateable value, not the gross value, of their houses. White said people considered the offer made by the new bill to be fairer than the current charges. The committee asked White if he had taken the trouble to compare what was in the newspapers with the existing charges of the Bristol Water Company. White said he knew the Bristol Water Company charges well, and had compared them. The difference lay, he said, in the gross instead of the rateable value and people thought their water would be cheaper if the bill was passed. Even if the water wasn't cheaper after the works, as the current situation wasn't working – with many residents unable to access clean water – it was a risk they were willing to take. In addition, passing the bill meant they would have to pay nothing for water closets and that baths would be cheaper, although he added there were not many of them in Horfield.

However, White reiterated to the committee that one of his complaints was that the cost of the service pipe had to be met by the home owners. The committee said this was the rule with all water companies, but White said he thought the laying of the service pipe should be free, just as it was with gas companies who installed pipes without charge. The committee impressed upon White that home owners picking up the bill for the pipes was common practice. White replied that the general feeling of the district was of unhappiness about this, especially as the roads were being broken up in order to install the pipes.

White then said to the committee, if you dip into a man's pocket, you begin to touch a very tender place with him.

Acton 1904, Maurice Kinch

People could not sleep at night as the bugs fell from the ceiling like a shower of rain upon the bed.

Bill to confer upon the Urban District Council of Acton further powers with regard to the supply of electricity and the improvement, health, local government, and finance of the district, and for other purposes.

Acton population growth

Year	Population
1801	461
1851	539
1901	593

Maurice Kinch was the chief sanitary inspector and inspector of nuisances of Acton Council in London. He gave evidence in Parliament on the Acton Improvement Bill in 1904 as he had experienced difficulties in getting premises cleaned under the power of that Act.

He explained that in the past two years he'd received around 150 complaints from all over Acton. Lodgers and home occupiers had contacted him to say they could not sleep at night as the bugs fell from the ceiling like a shower of rain upon the bed. Kinch had no power to deal with this nuisance himself as premises being dirty was not considered serious enough for the Public Health Act of 1890 to be enforced. Properties had to be 'injurious to health' and although a shower of bugs was certainly unpleasant and uncomfortable he didn't believe it endangered a person.

After presenting his case, a committee member observed, rather sarcastically, that in some parts of the country, they would say the ability to cohabit and survive with a house full of insects indicated that a person was remarkably healthy.

Kinch didn't believe the infestation made a house unfit for human habitation so he was unable to condemn it. He thought a house would have to be in a very bad state – damp and generally defective, dilapidated and ruinous for that to happen. But these houses were in a good state of preservation and the nuisance happened only at night when vermin (although not, he said, black beetles) would crawl out from the cracks in the floors and round the doors and the window sashes.

Another reason he was unable to condemn the properties was because, although there was an implied warranty under the Act of 1885 that a house must be reasonably fit for human habitation, this did not apply to unfurnished houses, which these were.

Additionally, despite recent legislation on this matter claiming to benefit the working classes, it had been applied only to houses over a certain value. There was no implied warranty in the case of an unfurnished house of this character, which was usually split into flats and lived in by the working classes. Each house might have three families, and while one might be clean, two might be dirty and thus the whole house would become infested. Plus, under section 76 of the Public Health Act, there was a clause that said a house, or any part of a house, should be fit for human habitation by persons of the working classes if the rent exceeded £8. In Acton rent was £8 but didn't exceed it.

Therefore, without the power to enforce change, on receiving a complaint from a resident, Kinch's only option was to contact the landlord. Some would agree to have the premises whitened or deep cleaned and others would refuse. Sometimes the tenants would take their furniture and leave and new tenants would move in, but find the place too verminous to even arrange their furniture and after two or three days, they would also leave.

Kinch needed the bill to be passed and for improvements to be made so that people could live comfortably in Acton while the bugs were forced to move out.

Lincoln 1915, James Crawshaw

One particular dyke was in a foul condition due to the build-up of glue that had flowed into the river for years.

23

Bill to authorise the mayor, aldermen, and citizens of the city of Lincoln, to acquire and extinguish the rights of the freemen of the city, and others in or in respect of the commons in and adjoining the city and to make provision for the management thereof; to provide and work trolley vehicles and motor omnibuses; to make further provision with regard to the supply of gas and electricity, and with regard to the health, local government, and improvement of the city, and for other purposes.

Lincoln population growth

1801	7,398
1851	17,536
1901	48,784

James Crawshaw was the last inspector of nuisances to give evidence in Parliament under the nuisances control legislation in 1915. He had been inspector of nuisances for Lincoln for ten years and prior to this had been the inspector for Halifax for five-and-a-half years. He gave evidence in the House of Commons on the Lincoln Corporation Bill with reference to sanitary issues for which he was responsible.

He was also responsible for meat and food, inspections of which he did in conjunction with the medical officer of health. It was their job to ensure that any food unfit for public consumption did not meet a single resident's plate or mouth.

Lincoln was a meat centre. The county of Lincolnshire was an agricultural district, where many animals were slaughtered, and their carcasses would be brought into the city to be distributed to other towns for food.

However, not every animal was slaughtered just for food. Sometimes it was because they had disease and their instant death would prevent it from spreading to other livestock. Nevertheless, sometimes these carcasses were knowingly sold on as food. Crawshaw told the committee of a recent incident known as 'the Liverpool case' when a diseased carcass was being brought into Lincoln surreptitiously. Butchers in the city were told, wrongly, that the carcass had been passed by an inspector, and on those grounds, they bought it.

This wasn't his only concern. In his position as inspector of sanitary nuisances, Crawshaw wanted more powers to force people, as well as businesses, to stop polluting the environment. Under the Public Health Act, it was necessary to give twenty-four hours' notice to the occupier of a house that a drain near their premises was to be opened for inspection. If it was found to be defective, the ground would be closed and a further notice served. Only on the default of the owner or occupier on the expiration of the notice could the local authority do their work. In the meantime the nuisance continued. The proposed bill would give inspectors such as Crawshaw the power to abate a nuisance at once, saving both time and money. In the case of combined drains, the saving was even greater than in the case of a single drain.

The 'combined drain system', when more than one house shared a drain, was used largely in the city. This meant Crawshaw would have several owners to consult before a problem could be abated, and several notices had to be served. However, a large number of the houses were owned by workmen and a closed up drain and no running water caused the workmen, who were unable to wash themselves or their tools, great inconvenience. It was really an insanitary condition of affairs.

Crawshaw wanted to know if Lincoln Corporation had experience in regard to this combined system, and was it aware of the number of owners Crawshaw had to deal with? He felt passing the proposed bill would give him the power to sort out these nuisances quicker and more effectively rather than waiting for each owner to agree and for the notice to expire.

He also drew the committee's attention to Clause 123 which regulated that solid matter should not to be thrown or conveyed into rivers or water courses. This was a problem in Lincoln and under current law, Crawshaw did not have the power to deal with the matter at all. This proposed clause would give him that power.

He referred to a case where there was a discharge from glue works, which started off as liquid before leaving a deposit that silted up. This waste matter had found its way into local dykes and streams into which the surface water drained. One particular dyke was in a foul condition due to the build-up of glue that had flowed into the river for years. Crawshaw couldn't say how much was in the water, or how much was discharged from the factory each day, only that it was continuous. Eventually the stream became blocked and stopped the water from flowing. Although Crawshaw accepted that the glue wasn't the only cause, he said this was the main reason for the blockage.

The only way to deal with it, explained Crawshaw, was to amend the clause to say not 'any solid matter' but 'any matter whatsoever' could be discharged into a stream. Presently, this glue manufacturer believed it had a right to discharge its liquid into the stream and Crawshaw wanted to be given the power to remove that right, or at least introduce restrictions.

Chapter 4

Water Supplies: Queues and Bad Smells

Leicester 1851, George Brown

> *If each of the 60,000 residents were to fetch a pint of water*
> *a day from it, the stream would be exhausted.*

Bill to amend the Leicester Waterworks Act 1847, to make certain alterations in the works, and to extend the period for completing such works and also to authorise an arrangement with the Local Board of Health for the Borough of Leicester.

Leicester population growth

1801	17,005
1851	65,405
1901	211,579

George Brown was an 82-year-old retired director of nuisances and former medical man from Leicester who had lived in the area virtually all his life and had left the position twelve months earlier due to infirmity. He gave evidence in the House of Lords on the Leicester Water Works Bill 1851.

Brown's view was that Leicester's water supply was defective and was becoming more of a nuisance as the population continued to grow at an alarming rate. The water quality was so bad that, in many instances, it was shocking to come into contact with it and the health of the town's residents was suffering as a result. When Brown had been in the medical profession some years before, typhus fever was rare and yet now it was extremely virulent. The people of Leicester were seldom without it and often, whole districts were affected by it.

Based on the number of houses in the area, Brown estimated that there were some 3,000 wells and pumps in Leicester and, of these, 2,000 were unusable. He never used pump water himself, and hadn't for years.

The committee turned its attention to the London Road Stream as there had been remarks about its condition. Brown said that, despite the fact it supplied the entire population of Leicester with water, which was some 60,000 people, it produced merely a dribble. He said that if each of the 60,000 residents were to fetch a pint of water a day from it, the stream would be exhausted.

The committee asked if the water supply had ever failed. Brown replied that it had failed many times, including that summer. It had failed at Queen Victoria's Coronation in 1838 when families needed water in order to cook for parties and celebrations.

Additionally, Brown told the committee that while there were sewers in Leicester, there was not a drop of water to flush them and without water, the sewerage of Leicester was deeply unsuitable and unclean.

Wolverhampton 1855, Richard Higgett

Higgett had actually threatened to summon the poor people to the magistrates as they were so filthy.

Bill for better supplying the Borough of Wolverhampton in the County of Stafford and its neighbourhood with water and for other purposes.

Wolverhampton population growth

1801	12,566
1851	49,985
1901	94,187

Richard Higgett gave evidence in the House of Commons on 15 May 1855 on the Wolverhampton New Water and the Wolverhampton Corporation Water bills. He lived at Wolverhampton, where he had been sub-inspector of nuisances in the employ of the Local Board of Health. This duty carried him into the 'lower' part of the town and made him intimately acquainted with the circumstances and conditions of the poor inhabitants of the town and well aware of their cleanliness, or want of cleanliness. Although he went all over the town, he said he was responsible for largely half of it – the west side.

Higgett had left the Local Board of Health on 31 December the year before on account of the surveyor making a report to the Sanitary Commission stating that they could dispense with Higgett's services and do the work themselves. He was, in effect, made redundant. However, he explained that he'd been employed by the Sanitary Board in Wolverhampton to make an inspection of the town on orders from London, not by the board.

Higgett's findings concluded that the water supply was very bad and it was often scarce. For half the town, particularly Stafford Street and Carraby Island, where the poorest, mainly Irish residents lived, only half the required quantity had been supplied since last summer and sometimes the condition was so bad, it was discoloured, like sand or marl. It was also so hard that it was unsuitable for washing. He estimated that nine out of ten houses in that area took their water from the Waterworks Company and thus it was the company's duty to solve this.

Higgett had complained about the water to a company official whose responsibility it was to turn on the water from the mains supply. The official – the turncock – said the company didn't have enough water to supply the town. Higgett told him it used to be better than this but the railway was taking so much that the residents were left without.

Higgett had actually threatened to summon the poor people to the magistrates as they were so filthy. They responded by saying this was because they regularly had no water for four or five days at a time. Their houses were smelly and nasty, and they couldn't clean them, their clothes or themselves.

Higgett told the committee that the previous summer, there had been scarcely a Saturday when the water was on at all in this half of town. In fact, he could only recall one Saturday in the whole of that summer when there had been any supply. Sometimes it was fit to drink and other times it wasn't. Higgett knew as he tasted it. It was often unpalatable and when it came from Dixon's works, it was coloured.

Mr Dixon had a reservoir, and the water that came to Wolverhampton from his works was so bad it was done away with. Bizarrely, the committee asked Higgett if it would make brandy and water, and he replied that it would not. It was totally undrinkable.

The committee asked him what the poor people did for water when they had no means of supply. He replied that they had to go without, or go a long way to the town pumps, but water there was only suitable for making tea, cooking or boiling potatoes.

There were many private pumps in Wolverhampton producing good water as people of means had felt their only option was to sink a well and have a pump of their own. Fortunately, these owners didn't often object to giving some to their poorer neighbours: they had given it to him many times in order to pass it on.

There was a dangerous element to this scarcity of water – what would happen in the event of a fire? Residents were worried that if a fire took, it could not be extinguished. It wasn't only the poorer people who were concerned. Higgett said one day there was a fire in a very respectable street in Wolverhampton – Falcon Street. It burned for three days without water.

Eccleshill 1858, William Booth

The water was very hard and impregnated with mineral and other matters so it was not suitable for domestic purposes.

Bill to extend the limits of the Bradford water work, and for authorising the construction of new and altered works, and for empowering the corporation of Bradford to borrow a further sum of money.

Eccleshill population growth

1801	1,351
1851	3,766
1901	8,666

William Booth was a district surveyor and inspector of nuisances under the Public Health Act. He lived in Eccleshill, a village beyond the boundary of the borough of Bradford in West Yorkshire. The bill under consideration by the House of Commons was, among other things, to supply Eccleshill with water.

At the time, Eccleshill had a population of 5,000. Although the Local Board of Health had existed for three years, during which time

Booth had been acting for it, it had failed to obtain any water supply despite applications and representations being made by local residents to the Corporation of Bradford asking for one. Booth knew the corporation wasn't compelled to provide water but hoped that this bill would change matters and make it compulsory.

An inspector had been sent by the General Board of Health to examine and report upon the condition of Eccleshill. It was discovered that the water was very hard and impregnated with mineral and other matters so it was not suitable for domestic purposes. Water had to come from elsewhere.

If the bill was passed, there were two ways that water could be supplied to the area – either in bulk or by specific distribution to each resident. Booth thought either way was suitable but that the town would prefer it in bulk as it would be more economical. He was assured the rate would be about sixpence per thousand gallons. The board would buy it and residents would pay the board in the form of taxes.

Booth and a gentleman named Dalby had now come before the Parliamentary Committee as a deputation from the Local Board of Health, authorized to represent the board's opinions and wishes.

Booth explained that, in his view, it was impossible for Eccleshill to supply itself with water independent of this proposed bill and that the only solution was for Bradford Corporation to take over the responsibility. He did not know how Eccleshill could be supplied otherwise. He thought it almost impossible that any other means might be found by which water could be supplied if this scheme was not sanctioned.

He argued that Eccleshill was growing and there was considerable manufacturing there, including four mills, which would benefit from a good supply of water. He believed that one mill carried its wool for a mile and a half, perhaps two, to find water. If this scheme was sanctioned by Parliament, he believed new mills would be built, bringing more industry and more jobs to the area.

He also said the provisions of the Removal of Nuisances Act could not be carried out without water. The Local Board of Health would not be able to do any good at all, or be of any use to the community unless they obtained this water supply. The properties and the people would remain unsanitary.

Under the proposed bill, water would be brought to near the Robin Hood Inn at Undercliffe, which was on the borders of Eccleshill.

The residents of Undercliffe petitioned at one time against the bill, or rather one clause, which they thought would give the authorities compulsory powers to make them pay a rate for water, even if the supply didn't reach them. They withdrew their opposition on the insertion of a proviso prohibiting the imposition of this rate if they went without water. Under the proposed legislation, the corporation would be bound to keep Eccleshill supplied with sufficient water.

Booth was in no way bound to contribute to the expenses of the Bradford Waterworks. Nor did his board intend to pay. Booth said he did not want to be granted the power to 'force' the corporation to provide water for his board. He said he wanted to have the 'privilege' to purchase it from them.

If the board did buy the water in bulk, Booth would provide for the pipes and other expenses. It would be necessary to borrow money in the first instance but then a rate would be levied on the residents, which would pay back the loan. There were no legal limits as to what that rate may be and Booth could charge what he wanted.

Booth had not made any estimate as to what this supply of water would cost. He acknowledged that he had been in office three years and had failed to do any sums but, as he pointed out, it was Eccleshill's only option and thus the cost was incidental. People needed water.

Rock Ferry 1859, Thomas Redhead

The poor people got their water from the pits belonging to the farmers, which was generally opaque and often filthy.

Bill for better supplying with water parts of the Parishes of Bebington and Woodchurch in the county of Chester and for other purposes.

Rock Ferry population growth

1801	143
1851	1,478
1901	2,971

In 1859, the incumbent of St Peter's Church at Rock Ferry, Cheshire, gave evidence in the House of Commons on the Wirral Water Bill.

Thomas Redhead had been curate of the parish for twenty-five years, incumbent for sixteen, was a freeholder there and one of the poor law guardians. He was also chairman of the Nuisances Removal Committee.

Redhead was well-acquainted with the area and believed he knew every person and every house. He referred the committee to two areas under his jurisdiction: one part of the parish that was inhabited by the wealthy and the other part – which was home to the poorest. The assessed value of the parish was about £12,900 a year.

Redhead told the committee Rock Ferry required a better supply of water. He said he knew that insufficient water in the richer area had prevented the land from being built on. He believed that, with a decent supply, it would have been done a long time ago as people had the means to build property there. As for the poorer part, there was virtually no water at all.

There was a hole in the middle of the township, which people called a well, but it contained little water and would regularly run dry. The poor people got their water from the pits belonging to the farmers, which was generally opaque and often filthy. Nevertheless, they paid a small sum for the liberty of going there. It was a considerable distance from their cottages, so unless they were up very early in the morning to empty two or three holes at the side of the road, which they frequently would do at 3am, they had to go about a quarter of a mile and carry it back in pails.

Redhead thought there was no doubt that the establishment of a waterworks company, as proposed by the bill, would be a benefit to the poor of the parish. Indeed, the whole population would benefit in every possible way. Redhead was so confident of this that he had become a company shareholder. He had not originally considered becoming a shareholder, but when he found there was some opposition to the bill, he bought fifty shares in order to show his support.

Rawmarsh 1870, John Rule

In one case the water smelt very much like rotten eggs.

Bill to extend the time for the compulsory purchase of lands and completion of the waterworks authorised by the Act relating to the Rotherham and Kimberworth Local Board of Health, and to authorise the said board to construct gas works and to purchase the undertaking of the Rotherham gas-light and coke company and to authorise various agreements with respect to water and gas and for other purposes.

Rawmarsh population growth

1801	1,101
1851	3,694
1901	14,567

John Rule was a district surveyor and inspector of nuisances for Rawmarsh near Rotherham in South Yorkshire. He gave evidence in the House of Commons on two bills in 1870. These were the Rotherham & Kimberworth Local Board of Health Bill 1870 and the Rotherham Gas & Rotherham & Kimberworth Local Board of Health Bill 1870.

He told the committee that he had been frequently called upon to examine the state of the water used by residents and found it to be full of all kinds of impurities. In some cases it was muddy, and in others it had a bad smell; in one case the water smelt very much like rotten eggs. Rule supposed chemists would call the stink sulphuretted hydrogen.

He said that four samples had been taken and carefully analyzed in Sheffield and up to thirty specimens, which included those taken from the contaminated water and those taken from the good, clean water that could be found in the area, had been tested by the medical officers of the parish. The result was that the water, believed to be the purest in the district, was indeed very pure. However, water taken from Candle Well, around half a mile from Rawmarsh, where poor people paid around three pence a week for just two pails for their tea – and sometimes paid people to carry it back for them – contained sewage.

The drainage, he said, was not satisfactory and could not be satisfactory until there was a water supply that allowed them to flush and drain the sewage from the water. It was pointless trying to do this now as they didn't have the means. The current system, he said, had isolated drains running into different streams. In some cases the drains had been so badly constructed that they had to be taken up and Rule found them stuffed full of solid matter. The sewage had regularly seeped into the wells used by the poor people.

Rule was satisfied that Rawmarsh would only get a water supply of its own if the bill was passed.

Finchley 1896, James Franklin

They stood at the entrance and urinated there, and it flowed across the footway.

Bill to confer further powers on the Urban District Council of Finchley in relation to their electricity undertaking, and to make further and better provision with regard to the improvement, health, local government, and finance of the district, and for other purposes.

Finchley population growth

1801	1,503
1851	4,126
1901	16,647

Edward James Franklin was sanitary inspector in Finchley in London, and gave evidence in the House of Commons on the Finchley Urban District Council Bill in 1908. His main concern was that a lack of lighting in refreshment rooms and public houses meant that people wouldn't use their lavatories and preferred to urinate on the lit streets instead.

He had spoken to occupiers of the licensed premises that failed to light their establishments and ordered them to do so, but found that even though most complied, this would lapse over time and when he re-inspected the premises, the lighting would cease to be in evidence.

On one occasion, he undertook a night inspection and of the twenty-two premises visited, thirteen were not lit.

This was one nuisance, but the real problem was that people would not enter a place of absolute darkness when they wanted to relieve themselves. Thus, they stood at the entrance and urinated there, and it flowed across the footway.

Whilst it was in the power of the licensing justices to attach conditions, Franklin told the committee he had no right to be heard before the licensing justices. There had been thirty-six cases in the last year but Franklin had been powerless to enforce any action.

Currently, the only remedy Franklin had was to take proceedings for nuisances under section 91 and the subsequent section of the Public Health Act. He had taken such proceedings under that section in many cases. However, he said that occupiers would take no notice of the communications addressed to them and he had to wait up to a month before he could get authority to serve a statutory notice and during that time, the nuisance continued.

Norwich 1907, Joseph Brooks

He found a uniform system of badness prevailed throughout, although some places were worse than others.

Bill to confirm certain provisional orders of the Local Government Board relating to Norwich and the county of London and Middlesex hereinafter designated as the Local Government Provisional Orders (No 13) Bill.

Norwich population growth

1801	35,633
1851	66,599
1901	100,815

Joseph Brooks, the chief inspector of nuisances in Norwich, gave evidence in the House of Lords in 1907 on the Local Government Provisional Orders (No. 13) Bill. He had been a health officer for nearly twenty years and was chiefly concerned with Catton and Sprowston, which were to the north of the centre. These parts of the town had about 515 houses and no system of sewerage whatsoever.

Brooks had never seen an area where the sanitary arrangements were so unsatisfactory. The general arrangement was drainage from the houses into cesspools, and the slops were then disposed of on the gardens. Brooks had found eighty-nine houses without any drainage arrangements, while a further twenty-one had refused to give him the information. A total of 405 houses had cesspools or dead wells: 110 in Catton and 295 in Sprowston.

With very few exceptions the cesspools were in close proximity to the houses. The majority were unventilated, and Brooks had reason to believe they were uncemented as well. This meant sewage would percolate into the subsoil.

Most of the cesspools he'd visited were full. He found the drains blocked in many places, and pools of sewage close to the houses.

In a number of cases, the tenants informed him that the cesspools had been full for months. The water supply for 290 of the houses came from the Norwich Waterworks Company, leaving 225 to obtain their water from pumps and draw wells. These were usually close to cesspools and there was no removal system whatsoever. Brooks found a lot of filth as well as offensive privy bins, which were often full and overflowing.

Prior to meeting the committee, Brooks had spent a number of days investigating the areas of greatest concern. He found a uniform system of badness prevailed throughout, although some places were worse than others. Of the fifteen houses on Wroxham Road, the first five on the left had heaps of manure and dirt in the yard. The cesspools were full, the drains were blocked and the privy pans were leaking. The tenant said he could get nothing done. Nearby roadways were also inches deep in mud and practically impassable.

Brooks also found houses that drained into cesspools. In Sydney Row, Wroxham Road there were twenty-eight houses and at the bottom of the row, the sewage flowed, almost daily, across the channel into the roadway. At the top of the row there was a cow shed and some pig sties, which were also in an insanitary condition, badly paved and drained.

This was repeated in many other areas around Wroxham Road. In Rackham's Fields, Brooks found local children had suffered from scarlet fever. The cesspools were full, the drains blocked, offensive water was standing in the yards and slops were being disposed of immediately against the houses. The residents had applied to Brooks for disinfectants, thinking that they would be able to deal with the situation that way. They couldn't. Wholesale change was needed.

Chapter 5

Water Supplies: Water Carts, Public Taps and Tadpoles in the Pipes

Liverpool 1847, Thomas Fresh

People had no time to get the water and they were quarrelling over who should get it first.

Act for better suppling with water the Borough of Liverpool and the neighbourhood thereof, and for authorising the mayor, aldermen, and burgesses of the said Borough to purchase the Liverpool and Harington Waterworks and Liverpool Waterworks.

Liverpool population growth
1801	77,765
1851	376,065
1901	704,134

Thomas Fresh, inspector of nuisances of Liverpool Corporation for the past twelve years, gave evidence in the House of Lords on the Liverpool Corporation Waterworks Bill in 1847. He had already given evidence on the same bill in the House of Commons.

The corporation employed him to collect samples of the water for a Dr Lyon Playfair, a chemist to the Museum of Geology, which was based in the Department of Woods and Forests. Fresh duly procured samples from different brooks and streams, bottled them and delivered them to Dr Playfair at the town hall.

Fresh was well aware that the water supply was beyond par due to the many complaints he received, especially from those in the poorer districts. He also found the positioning of the toilet cisterns in these rundown courts and houses a matter of concern.

In many places, the courts were so narrow, it was impossible to install cisterns over the privies and they had to be placed underneath the flagstones. In some cases, the filth from the courts drained into them. The public tap in these premises was also not fit for purpose as it only remained on for a short time, no more than ten or fifteen minutes. People had no time to get the water and they were quarrelling over who should get it first.

Fresh explained to the committee that fitting the district with a proper water supply would mean altering the houses in order to fit the cisterns above the privies. Fresh thought that, considering many of these courts were just 3ft wide, it would be more sanitary to pull them down altogether and build new properties with more room. However this, he said, would result in uprooting a great number of residents – possibly one third of all the town's inhabitants.

Consett and Knitsley 1860, George Thompson

The good water seemed to be reserved for the factories and foundries while the people were left with the worst.

Bill for better supplying with water the inhabitants of Consett and other districts in the county of Durham.

Consett and Knitsley population growth

1801	754
1851	2,774
1901	10,521

George Thompson was the superintendent of police and inspector of nuisances in the township of Consett and Knitsley in County Durham. He gave evidence in the House of Commons in 1860 on the Consett District Water Bill.

There was a lack of good water in the district, which was a hub of industry and housed a few thousand people, many of whom were poor labourers and miners. However, the good water seemed to be reserved for the factories and foundries while the people were left with the worst.

Almost all the water had to be obtained from Dell's Well, which belonged to Mr Dolphin who had let it to Mr Little for £1 a week. Little carried the water from there with three water carts, for which Thompson thought Dolphin levied a very high charge of one pence for four gallons.

The water in the well was not plentiful at any time but in dry seasons was dangerously scarce. On these occasions, Mr Little would be forced to travel further afield to get water anywhere he could find. In Thompson's view, this water was inferior to the water obtained from Dell's Well, even though that wasn't considered to be very good as it was rather hard.

However, it was better than the alternatives. A man called Bolan supplied water to the district which he got from a pump out of Adamson's field, near the Consett ironworks, but it was peaty and not fit for drinking. Another supplier, a man named Mossop, got his water from the Carr House quarry, but this was exceptionally dire. Hard, discoloured and with a bad taste, it was procured from a place where a great number of dogs and cats had been thrown to be drowned.

Despite the dreadful quality, all this water was still paid for by the poor people of Consett who could not afford any better. The very poorest had to purchase their water from Boggle Hole pond. Water from there was the worst in town. The refuse water from Crook Hall works ran into Boggle Hole, as did a portion of the sewage of the town of Lydgate. Dead dogs were also thrown in there. Despite this, the inhabitants of the district would go there to bathe in summer time, and some even drank from it.

Thompson had his own house and many times had refused to drink the water that his less fortunate neighbours, usually the labourers, were compelled to drink. Thompson believed drinking the water was bad for morale and affected the health of the residents. The drains and sewers remained unflushed and if there was a fire, the only water could be brought by water cart from Boggle Hole.

However, it wasn't true to say the area did not have a strong supply of good, safe water as there was a pumping engine by Boggle Hole. The water was pumped up to within 200yds of Berry Edge, where it came into a small pond. This pump was maintained by the Derwent Iron Company so they could pump it into their works, but not to the people. They had to get it out with buckets, or any way they could, which was not conducive to healthy living and certainly not appropriate in the event of a fire.

Similarly, the Stockton and Darlington Railway, which passed through the district, had its own reservoir, which was supplied from the springs at Felden Head and produced very good water. The problem was the needs of manufacturing and industry were being prioritized over the needs of the people.

Thompson knew a little about the works proposed in the bill and thought they would benefit the town a great deal. Residents were very much in favour of the works and were anxious for the bill to be passed. The population was increasing rapidly and new factories, dependent on the growing iron trade, were springing up. The Berry Edge and Consett Ironworks, the Cook Hall Ironworks and the Bradley Ironworks had all been built in the past eighteen years, and whereas the jobs were welcome, it was unacceptable for hard-working labourers and the families to not have clean drinking water and be able to wash themselves and their clothes properly. The area was modernizing and the water supply had to follow suit. The current situation was unsatisfactory and was only going to get worse.

Chepstow 1887, William Williams

> *He did not wish to act like a 'dog-in-the-manger', but thought it was very important that he should get as ample a supply of water as possible.*

Bill to confirm certain Provisional Orders made by the Board of Trade under the Electric Lighting Acts 1881 and 1888, relating to Bedlingtonshire, Chepstow (Urban and Rural), Cowes, Hitchin, Morpeth, Ashington, Newbiggin-by-the-Sea and Morpeth (Rural), Pokesdown, Slough and Datchet, Stevenage, Tadcaster and District, Trefriw and certain districts and parishes in the West Riding in the county of York hereinafter designated as the Electric Lighting Provisional Orders (no 7) Bill, and for other purposes.

Chepstow population growth
1801	2,080
1841	4,332
1901	3,067 [sic]

Reverend William Williams was the chairman of the Rural District Council of Chepstow, in Monmouthshire in Wales. He was a clergyman of the Church of England and Clerk in Holy Orders of Portskewett Rectory as well as being inspector of nuisances and a district and council surveyor. He knew the Chepstow district very well as he had worked there for seventeen years and had spent the earlier part of his life there. He gave evidence to the committee on the Electric Lighting Provisional Orders (No. 7) Bill 1887.

Williams told the committee that the constant pumping at the Severn Tunnel had a considerable effect on the water supply of the district. It had drained every well in his parish and other parishes to the west, in the direction where the waterworks were being formed. It had exhausted the sink holes and reduced the amount of water going down the Neddern, which was a tributary of the River Severn.

Williams told the committee that the parish of Portskewett and Caldicot depended upon the Severn Tunnel for its water supply. The district got its drinking water entirely from the Great Western pumping station. If fresh water was desired, it had to be obtained from the Neddern stream, so the reduction of water there was highly undesirable.

The Great Western pumping station was in the parish, hardly a mile off. The district council had to supply the pipe, but Great Western pumped it up. Williams thought they had acted very generously as the charge for the water was two pence per thousand gallons. That did not, however, supply the whole of the district, only the Severn Tunnel portion. Williams told the committee the water was drinkable. He himself drank a great deal of it, and he did not think he looked as if he was taking very many Epsom salts. Williams thought about a third of his local area was supplied by the Great Western. The part of the district not supplied by the Great Western pumping station relied partly on the few wells that were left and on the Neddern stream.

Williams said that recently water had been running dry and there was a great fear that if the water from the Neddern was interfered with any more, the supply would be even shorter. The residents were concerned.

The committee considered the pumping by the Great Western. One of the objections had been that, at any time, the River Severn might find its way into the tunnel and flood the place, spoiling the water. Williams replied that he was not a geologist and therefore, would not like to give an opinion.

Williams believed that the quantity of water being actually used by the Great Western was about 20 million gallons a day. That was being continuously taken out from subterranean sources and put into the Severn. The Great Western was supplying some 3,000 people. A smaller number were dependent on the Neddern, a population of more than 1,000.

Williams had noticed the effect of the pumping of the Great Western had been continuous and cumulative. His opinion was that the quality of the water supplied from the Neddern wasn't as good as it was before the Great Western pumping station had opened. Additionally, the supply in the Neddern had been decreasing but the population had been increasing (Williams' own parish had grown from 200 to 1,180).

Williams had also found that when the volume of the stream lessened, fresh sink holes were opened, which would take the water away.

Williams was asked whether, as chairman of the board, he thought it unadvisable that the water supply should be touched. He replied that he thought it should. He did not wish to act like a 'dog-in-the-manger', but thought it was very important that he should get as ample a supply of water as possible.

Meriden 1907, Samuel Bretherton

Two of the houses there were without water for four or five months of the year.

Bill to confer further powers on the mayor, aldermen, and the citizens of the City of Coventry in relation to their water undertaking; to authorise the supply to them of water by the lord mayor, aldermen, and citizens of the City of Birmingham; to extend the area of supply under the Coventry Electric Lighting Order 1891, and for other purposes.

Meriden population growth

1801	8,904
1851	11,260
1901	11,346

Samuel Bretherton was a surveyor and inspector of nuisances for the Meriden Rural District Council, Coventry. He gave evidence in the House of Lords in 1907 on the Coventry Corporation Water Bill. He told the committee he had been connected with Meriden for some thirty-three years and knew all about Meriden and its five parishes, through which the water main proposed by the bill would travel.

Presently, two of the parishes were receiving no water at all. One parish covered 2,854 acres, and had a population of 231 with forty-six houses. Another of the parishes covered 2,568 acres and had a population of 202 and forty-two houses. Both parishes should be supplied by pipes from Shustoke.

The committee turned its attention to the parish of Maxstoke. Bretherton said two of the houses there were without water for four or five months of the year. The committee observed that that spoke for itself – it was not desirable. Those two houses were inhabited by forty people. They did, however, fare better than their neighbouring house where four people lived and which received no water at all. Two other neighbours received water but it was not wholesome.

Further on, towards Maxstoke Church, two houses were supplied by a spring which ran through an open ditch for a quarter of a mile.

The aqueduct went on into the village of Great Packington where the water had been condemned by the county analyst because it was totally unfit for use. Then came a house with no supply of water at all. The wells were enclosed and the people living there had to fetch their water from about 200yrds away.

He told the committee that the village of Maxstoke was owned by a Mr Featherstone. Maxstoke Castle was supplied by a private arrangement but the ordinary people fetched their water by cart from the waterworks at Whitacre, at least one-and-a-half miles away.

Bretherton had never had any communication with Mr Featherstone about the water. However, Lord Aylesford who owned most of the property in Great Packington had taken action, so that the residents only had to go 200yds to fetch their water. Bretherton acknowledged that a decent water supply was a great concern to Lord Aylesford. His agents had been in communication with Bretherton and were anxious to get the water to the people. Mr Featherstone was not as attentive.

Bretherton then told the committee that there were three other parishes which had a right to take a supply from the North Warwickshire Company but none of these were being supplied with water.

Bretherton said a main had been laid in Meriden by the water company and he had every reason to suppose there would be a supply of water there. He thought it would be practical to tap this main at any point and get a water supply to every house that wanted it (although not every house wanted mains water as they did not have cisterns and did not want to have them installed) along the road. He felt this was the only solution.

The committee disagreed and wondered whether, instead of taking water direct from the main supply, it would be sufficient to fill a week's worth of water in a tank and construct a storage reservoir in which to keep it. Bretherton said this would be too costly and residents didn't want to pay. Instead he wanted to install seven connections to the main and have a constant supply.

The committee, still keen to find a suitable alternative, asked Bretherton whether it would be cheaper to stop the sources of local pollution rather than lay new mains. He replied that in some cases a large amount of money had been spent trying to improve the supply with no great success. At Maxstoke Castle, hundreds of pounds had been spent, and the water was still bad. For Bretherton, the only way of getting a wholesome supply of water throughout the district was to install a mains supply of water.

Caerphilly 1911, Evan Morgan

Often, if the taps were removed, they would find frogs' body parts and dead tadpoles clogging up the pipe.

Bill to constitute a Water Board for the Rhymney Valley with power to acquire certain water undertakings and works, to construct new works and to supply water; to make provision with respect to the establishment of a joint committee of the board and the Corporation of Merthyr Tydfil for certain purposes of the Act, and for other purposes.

Caerphilly population growth

1801	4,666
1851	9,460
1901	13,835

Evan Thomas Morgan had been the inspector of nuisances in Caerphilly in Wales for seventeen years when he gave evidence in the House of Lords on the Rhymney Valley Water Bill in 1911.

Morgan told the committee that the least satisfactory water supply in his district was in Senghenydd and Aber. The former was the location for the Universal Colliery supply and the colliery was using so much water, there wasn't enough left for the residents and much of what was available wasn't fit for purpose.

The colliery had been opened by the Universal Steam Coal Company in the 1890s and in 1913, two years after this hearing, it would be the scene of Britain's worst mining disaster when 436 men and boys died in an explosion. A previous explosion in 1901 had resulted in the deaths of eighty-two but recommendations from the resulting inquiry had not been implemented by 1913.

Morgan told the committee that the water sources in the area were in a very poor condition. The one at Gwern-y-Milwr, which was owned by the Gwern-y-Milwr Land Company, was filthy and always liable to pollution. Another source, the reservoir at Maesdiofal Farm, belonging to the Gwern-y-Milwr Land Company, was also open to pollution and the fence around it was in a dilapidated state.

Morgan had visited the reservoir on 17 February 1910 with an engineer, Mr Raikes, who specialized in sewerage systems and had even written a book on sewage disposal. Morgan told the committee that at the top end of the reservoir he had noticed a lot of human excreta, horse manure and sheep manure. He also found the carcasses of two dogs, which he took out and buried. Furthermore, the side nearest to the road was being used as a privy. Morgan did not regard the water from that source as being suitable for a domestic supply at all. Additionally, the reservoir was only half full and yet this was the wet season. About seventy houses drew their supplies from this source.

Morgan told the committee he'd taken samples from a number of houses in his area and they were all unfit for domestic purposes. One water source on a mountainside led into a small tank and from there into a lower tank. There was merely an attempt at filtration and, in Morgan's view, the whole of the ground was open to pollution before it entered the tank. In another case, a mechanical filter was in place but not all the water passed through the filter.

He then produced a sample bottle, which he had filled from a tap in a house belonging to a Mr John Wood. The house was on the Park Knead estate of Mr Matthias and the water came from a small stream. The source was small but not satisfactory as it often ran short in dry weather, although it did not fail completely. The committee asked what were the black things they could see. Morgan said they were tadpoles. Morgan said he often got complaints about the service pipes of the houses being choked up with tadpoles. Often, if the taps were removed, they would find frogs' body parts and dead tadpoles clogging up the pipe, which would have to be cleared out.

Chapter 6

Human Waste: Night Soil and Cesspools

Liverpool 1853, Thomas Fresh

*Using Liverpool's manure to fertilize local land would mean
it could be brought into profitable occupation.*

Fresh was giving evidence on several bills grouped together for
consideration.

Liverpool population growth

1801	77,765
1851	376,065
1901	704,134

Thomas Fresh, the inspector of nuisances in Liverpool, gave evidence
in the House of Commons in 1853. His job included responsibility for
a task of great importance to the borough of Liverpool – the removal of
sewage or night soil. He told the committee that the night soil ought to
be taken away at as cheap a rate as possible.

At the time Fresh was giving evidence, night soil was being taken
away and left on the coast between Southport and Liverpool. By dumping
it there, it was turning the barren land into fertile soil, which was also
described as 'hungry' soil.

Without doubt, there had been a mutual advantage to this procedure
as the people of Liverpool benefited from its removal and the soil was
thriving. Around 20,000 tons were being disposed of this way but the
problem arose from the cost of getting it there. It was so significant
that it almost outweighed the advantage of it being removed. Fresh,
himself a landowner who had bought around 50 acres from Mr Blundell
of Ince, had used around 1,000 tons of soil for his own fertilization

purposes this spring. He thought Liverpool, and neighbouring Formby, could benefit from using the soil themselves and not paying for it to be transported elsewhere.

There was, he told the committee, a large quantity of land in the direction of Formby, which lay in a quite uncultivated state. He wasn't sure how many thousands of acres there were, although Mr Blundell had told him he had access to about 5,000 acres there. Using Liverpool's manure to fertilize local land would mean it could be brought into profitable occupation. Presently, the land grew only poor, rank grass, which fed a few hungry rabbits.

Yeovil 1864, Robert Williams

The matter in the cesspool was soaking through the wall into the wells.

Bill for the regulation of the municipal corporation of the Borough of Yeovil in the County of Somerset and for the extension of the boundaries of the said Borough and for the improvement of the said Borough.

Yeovil population growth

1801	2,740
1851	7,844
1901	9,806

Robert Thomas Williams, the inspector of nuisances and town surveyor of Yeovil, gave evidence in the House of Commons on the Yeovil Improvement Bill in 1864.

The committee asked Williams about the drainage in Yeovil to which he replied there was very little and it was all private. The drains that were there were of poor quality, mostly dug out of the earth, with a few stones at the side and some large flat stones on the top, without mortar and covered in flagstones. The bottom was generally muddy soil and, in some cases, there were cuts formed in the soil from which land waters were flowing through. There were also a great many cesspools, 10 or 12ft above the tops of the wells. Consequently, the matter in the cesspools was soaking through the wall into the wells.

The drains were only around 2ft below the surface of the road, which made it difficult for them to be flushed. Williams knew of one that was just 6 inches (ins) below the ground. There wasn't enough water to flush them anyway – at present, he said as he faced the committee, there was no water at all – and without an ample supply of water, a drainage system was never going to work. Williams told the committee that a public meeting had been held to discuss the insufficient drainage and the want of water.

Williams knew the poorer class of houses in Yeovil – he had visited them all, house to house. They were supplied with water from wells sunk 25ft or more, but it was merely surface drainage. The small amount of water they could access was very hard and much of it could not be used.

Currently, the improvement commissioners had no power whatsoever over the private drains and this was a great inconvenience as it prevented a regular public drainage system from being built. They also had no funds to make improvements but this bill would give them the funds needed, and Williams was keen to see it passed.

Whitehaven 1899, John Smith

The beck was only a few steps across the road, so it was easier to throw the night soil in there.

Bill to confer further powers on the Corporation of Whitehaven with respect to their water and electric lighting undertakings; to extend the borough of Whitehaven; to consolidate the rates of the borough, and simplify the collection thereof, and for other purposes.

Whitehaven population growth
1801	8,742
1841	14,190
1901	21,488

John Smith, the inspector of nuisances in Whitehaven in Cumbria, gave evidence in the House of Lords on the Whitehaven Corporation Bill in 1899. He told the committee that most, but not all, sewers in Whitehaven were connected with the main sewers. Of the 295 houses, about twenty-five were not connected.

A great many of these houses had water closets: 165 had one for each house, forty-two houses shared with their neighbour and three houses had the use of one closet between them. The remaining sixty had pails or privies, and the ashes were removed every day by cart. This was well advertised with the distribution of handbills and public notices alerting residents to the time the cart would pass through their neighbourhood. If the people refused to comply and leave their ashes outside so they could be carted away, Smith would impose penalties. He also served notices if pails were being put in the streets.

Smith told the committee that the village was divided into two areas for sewerage. The principal sewage farm was about 4½ acres and drained 187 water closets. The second sewage farm, the Chapel House Sewage Farm, was around 1½ acres and drained fifty-eight houses.

Smith explained that the liquid sewage came down a main carrier and was distributed and left in horizontal carriers, where it would be allowed to settle and solidify. They were worked alternately – the plot at the high side for a day or two, and then the plot lower down. When the liquid matter had percolated through the soil, the solid matter was dug out and carted away by the farmer. The percolation in the soil at the lower end of the field was, to all appearances, perfectly pure.

The committee then asked what happened to the rainfall from the roofs of the houses in the streets. Smith replied that the Hensingham Authority had carried out an efficient system, which kept the sewage and rainfall apart. Three streams carried away the rainfall whereas the sewage went to the land. That was a maxim devised by the officers of the Local Government Board: put the sewage to the land and the rainfall to the stream and keep all possible rainfall from the sewage. But the method did not work perfectly.

Smith was aware of five houses at Beck Bottom, whose slop water and night soil went into Snebra Beck. The main sewer passed within 2yds of the properties, only one of which had a water closet while two had an ash pit and privy in the garden.

The committee was also aware that close to the highway at the entrance to Beck Bottom, there was a slaughterhouse, in which two cattle, eight to twelve sheep and several pigs were killed weekly. All of the blood and tripe dressings were discharged through an open grating right into the beck, and there was a purple, almost scarlet, foam at times on the beck, which ran down into the harbour. The discolouration could be seen for a considerable distance.

The committee expressed concern of such matter finding its way into the harbour. In reference to the houses in Beck Bottom, Smith said one water closet was not sufficient for five houses with families. People had to go the whole length of the row before they could arrive at the water closet. The beck was only a few steps across the road, so it was easier to throw the night soil in there. He was asked why it wasn't carted away. He said he didn't know if it was removed on occasion but he had personally witnessed the throwing of the night soil into the beck when he had gone to visit the area after being alarmed at the discolouration of the flowing water.

The inference, said Smith, was that they did this all the time, although he could not say for sure.

He agreed that it wasn't necessary but he could see why they did it. They certainly knew about the ash cart due to the amount of advertising in place to publicize it.

He added that Snebra Beck was already polluted as the workhouse (which was not under the corporation's jurisdiction so Smith had no power to prevent it from happening) and the cemetery also drained into it. Smith agreed with a committee member that it was little wonder that there was a large amount of excrementitious matter in the harbour.

Chapter 7

Human Waste: Water Closets and Shrimps

Cheltenham 1879, James Long

Close by was a butcher's house and he saw offal, closet soil and all manner of filth was coming from that drain.

Bill for empowering the Mayor, Aldermen and Burgesses of the Borough of Cheltenham to acquire the undertaking of the Cheltenham Waterworks Company and for supplying with water the Borough of Cheltenham and other places and for other purposes.

Cheltenham population growth

1801	3,076
1851	35,051
1901	41,136

James Long had been inspector of nuisances for Cheltenham, Gloucestershire, for three years when he gave evidence on the Cheltenham Corporation Water Bill in 1879.

One year earlier, Long had gone to Upton where he had taken a boat down the River Severn, past the town. It wasn't long before he saw several private drains running from houses, which had closet soil oozing from them and into the river. He ordered the boatman to pull close to the culvert but he was unable to get within 8 or 10yds of it on account of the mud and dirt in his way.

Close by was a butcher's house and he saw offal, closet soil and all manner of filth coming from that drain. He also observed it overflowing from the neighbouring pubs, The King's Head, The Plough and The Wheatsheaf, as well as Kent's Liquor Vaults.

Leeds. Expanding industrial production pumped out pollution until the Clean Air Act of the 1960s.

An overcrowded London slum.

Children generate washing in Birmingham.

Building a sewer in Fleet Street, London, 1845.

Kensal Rise, London. Housing and industry overlap.

A steam train travels between houses, pumping out smoke.

The interior of a dirty, overcrowded house in Leeds, c.1915.

'Showers' of bed bugs kept people awake in Acton, London.

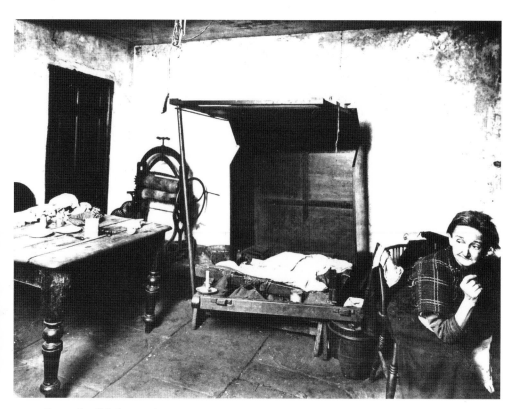

Everyday life in Leeds.

The Great Northern London Cemetery had very poor drainage.

Slaughterhouses attracted attention from inspectors of nuisances. Leeds.

Above left: Even Queen Victoria was not immune to the 'Great Stink'. *Punch*, 1861.

Above right: Joseph Bazalgette's sewering of London was arguably one of the greatest contributions by any civil engineer to daily life in London.

The boatman did not think it was anything exceptional. Long asked him how often the river was cleaned and he said every summer at low water time, when 70 to 90 tons of dirt was removed. The boatman added that, in his opinion, there were 50 or 60 tons of dirt in the river as he and Long bobbed along.

Long wanted to ascertain what proportion of the houses of Upton drained into the river, so as soon as he left the boat, he sent for the most renowned builder in the town, Mr John Crump. Crump said there was not a man in the town who knew the sewerage system better than he did and he told Long that aside from eight or twelve houses, which drained into Molly Dobbs' ditch, all the rest of Upton drained into the Severn.

Upton's population was around 2,500 people, with an average of five people to a house. This meant around 500 houses were draining into the Severn. There was, Long discovered, nowhere else they could drain to as there were no sewage works of which he was aware. With no sewage works, those not on the banks could not drain into the Severn, and instead drained into old culverts.

The committee was not impressed. They asked Long if he had ever seen a place where there was no sewage works and where all or most of the sewage ran into the river. He acknowledged that where there was no sewage works the ordinary rule was to drain into cesspools, which was what they did. However, the cesspools held the solids but the liquid leaked out.

Long told the committee that, despite being the inspector of nuisances, he had not been aware that the local board was compelled to dispose of its sewage so as to do no harm. He believed the board of Upton-on-Severn had not been doing anything of the sort.

Pudsey 1881, Joseph Town

Bradford landlords now had to go to the expense of having water closets provided.

Bill to enable the Mayor, Aldermen and Burgesses of the Borough of Bradford in the West Riding of the county of York to construct and maintain additional works for the storage and supply of water, to enlarge the time for making waterworks already authorised, to effect public improvements, to enlarge the borough, for municipal, sanitary and School Board purposes, and for other purposes.

Pudsey population growth

1801	4,422
1851	11,603
1901	14,907

Joseph Town, inspector of nuisances for Pudsey, between Leeds and Bradford in Yorkshire, gave evidence in the House of Commons on the Bradford Water and Improvement Bill in 1881. He had been living in Pudsey for 'thirty-five years and better', and had been inspector of nuisances for eight years. It had been a full-time job and he made his inspections at regular periodic intervals.

Town was asked if he ever went to nearby Tyersal, and he said he did and that it was in an insanitary condition. He thought there was only one water closet in Tyersal, with the other houses owning ash pits. It was part of Town's responsibilities to see to the removal of matter from these ash pits. A large number of houses in Tyersal drained into Bradford but recently, 580 houses had begun to drain from Bradford into the Tyersal Beck.

This was a reversal of fortune because previously 150 to 200 houses from Bradford used to drain into Tyersal. However, as Bradford landlords now had to go to the expense of having water closets provided, Bradford residents were now complaining to Town about the filthy state of Tyersal.

Bradford's town clerk had complained of the sewage being sent into their district, and the board hoped that some amicable arrangement could be made. Town asked the clerk if he could make any arrangement whereby the sewage might be admitted into their sewers, and he said he believed the town council was indisposed to take the thing in hand. Subsequently this bill had been introduced, which prevented the local board taking steps until they saw the issue of it.

Town brought up the problem of emptying the ash pits and privies. As a rule, the landlord paid a rate for the removal of these ash pits to be done by the board. However, Town did not have enough staff to carry out this job, but he pointed out that nearby Pudsey was an agricultural district, and the farmers there were happy to take the contents of the ash pits and the privies. There was also a number of night soil men who would take it away for a trifle cost. Town was asked if he superintended that, to see that no nuisance was created. He said he could not always be present, but he had issued a warning that he would take steps if the regulations and the bye-laws were not observed.

Town was aware that Pudsey Local Board was also sending an amount of sewage into Bradford. Bradford asked Pudsey's permission to make a sewer through part of Pudsey, coming around again into the Bradford system. The whole of the drainage of Tyersal used to come into Pudsey, but it was diverted by the railway in 1854 and so it drained mainly into Bradford. Town was obliged to divert Pudsey's sewage at an increased expense, in order for it to go down the Tyersal Beck.

In July, the board had granted Town permission to install a sewer along what was called Lodom Lane, to take a portion of the sewage of Bradford into its own drain. This new work would lead from Bradford through Pudsey and come back again into Bradford.

Bristol 1887, John Kirley

When a bucket of water was drawn from the tap in his presence, he strained a large tea cup full of shrimps.

Bill for incorporating Bristol Consumers Water Company, and empowering them to construct Waterworks and supply water, and for other purposes.

Bristol population growth

1801	40,814
1851	137,228
1901	439,466

John Kirley was inspector of nuisances for the district of Bristol Urban Authority and gave evidence in the House of Lords on the Bristol Consumers Water Bill in 1887. He told the committee he had fourteen years' experience of sanitary work for Bristol.

Speaking generally, he found the houses occupied by the artisans and working classes were badly provided for in the way of water closets. They were without the means of flushing, except by buckets of water thrown down by hand. Consequently, he usually found them dirty, often filthy. Kirley was sure the committee would not want him to go into a number of very unsavoury details.

In the courts in the city, the tenants usually got their supply of water from one communal tap. Where that was the case, privies would not be flushed at all unless the sanitary authority sent men round to flush them with buckets.

In the better class of house, the servants' privies were also very bad and had no means of flushing, except by hand. In most cases, Kirley had recommended to the owners that a supply of water for flushing should be obtained but had been told the expense was too great and they simply could not afford it. He heard this from numerous masters and mistresses.

There were, Kirley told the committee, houses in the city supplied only with well water but he'd had to close many wells due to the state of the water. In each case, Kirley had compelled people to obtain a supply of water from the Bristol Consumers Water Company but found they were reluctant to do so on account of the high charges the company imposed. Consequently, people would not act except under compulsion. The committee's chairman observed slyly that they probably never would, especially if they could get a thing for nothing.

Kirley observed that during the previous summer, there had been several complaints made to him about the condition of the water. It was often turbid and sometimes it contained fish. Kirley went to one house and when a bucket of water was drawn from the tap in his presence, he strained a large tea cup full of shrimps.

It was his duty to report to the medical officer, Dr Davis, if there was anything that needed rectifying that he could not get done himself. Whereas Kirley wouldn't go as far to say he'd reported on the condition of the water, he did, from time to time, report on the insanitary conditions of the water closets due to the insufficient supply of water. He said they were dirty and that they had been installed by landlords cheaply, as they wanted to get their rent with as little expense as possible.

Bolton 1905, William Bland

He thought there ought to be no charge for the first water closet in a house.

Bill to authorise the Mayor, Aldermen, and Burgesses of the Borough of Bolton to construct an Aqueduct and other Works in connexion with the intended Wayoh Reservoir; and to make further Provisions for the Regulation of the Borough.

Bolton population growth

1801	20,893
1841	58,444
1901	168,215

William Bland, inspector of nuisances for Bolton in Lancashire, gave evidence in the House of Commons in 1905 on the Bolton Corporation Bill. He discussed with the committee regulations to be made under the Bolton Corporation Act 1872.

The committee had been given figures for the cost of water supply, which came to exactly sixpence per 1,000 gallons. Bland explained that Bolton Corporation was paying four times that, although the more the council took, the less it paid. There was no advantage whatsoever in paying annually as accounts were sent quarterly.

With regard to water closets, Bland was asked whether, in his judgement, the charge that was levied on the first water closet in a house was too high. He said yes and added that he thought there ought to be no charge for that. That was the practice in Manchester. By charging five shillings for the first water closet, Bolton Corporation was, in Bland's view, preventing sanitation from being improved. He said the charge was excessive and people were reluctant or unable to pay.

He was asked if he thought the charge prevented the adoption of a water carriage system capable of dealing with human excrement. Bland said it had hindered the conversion of privy middens into water closets in his district, and no doubt in other districts. The regulations, which had been intended to prevent waste and loss of water, were not in the interests of consumers.

There was another issue with repairs. If a pipe burst, residents had to send for the corporation's plumber to give notice to have the water turned off. The plumbers would then have to give notice to the corporation waterman to have the water turned off, and they would normally charge one shilling before the repair could be made. In Manchester, for example, the resident could turn the water off themselves and have the repair fixed at once. Due to the regularity in which problems happened and pipes burst (Bland knew of twenty cases in Clifton alone) it was a costly and inconvenient issue.

Chapter 8

Human Waste: Sewage

Hyde 1862, Matthew Maiden

There were streets of houses 300yds long with open cesspools 2ft, 4ft and 8ft deep, and nearly full to the top with excrementitious matter, urine and other filth.

Bill to protect the Waters of the Mersey and Irwell and of certain of their Tributaries from certain Obstructions.

Hyde population growth

1801	1,063
1851	11,569
1901	23,668

In 1862, Matthew Maiden, inspector of nuisances for Hyde, Cheshire, gave evidence in the House of Lords on the Mersey, Weaver, Irwell etc Protection Bill. He began by having to point out to the committee where Hyde was on a map, and told them it was a great manufacturing area situated on the River Tame, one of the confluents of the Mersey.

Maiden said Hyde was insanitary as there was no proper drainage and there was a delay in removing night soil from houses for the neighbourhood had no need – no land needed cultivating. There were streets of houses 300yrds long with open cesspools 2ft, 4ft and 8ft deep, and nearly full to the top with excrementitious matter, urine and other filth. The ashes from the ash pits were thrown into streams.

Maiden explained that in a bid to sort this out, he had joined forces with an organization called the Eureka Company. The Eureka Company had discovered a need for the night soil and said they would collect it. Quickly, the contents of the cesspools were made into good land and there was a cask placed there for the deposit of ashes twice a week, supplied with a deodorized box. There was no smell whatsoever – it was as clean as any gentleman's stable yard. The ashes were taken away, ground up and used in mortar for building roads and railways tracks. In fact, a large contractor had a great demand for the ashes and paid as much as half a crown per cart load. The manure from the night soil was also being used and they were getting around £7 per ton for it.

Maiden was pleased with the work carried out by the Eureka Company and felt that the area had benefitted greatly from their partnership. The committee told Maiden the same thing had been tried in Cardiff but it did not pay. Maiden had a success story on his hands.

Beverley 1881, John Vickers

He said the people were not nearly so dirty as they had been described.

Bill for better supplying with water Beverley and its neighbourhood in the East Riding to the County of York.

Beverley population growth

1801	5,001
1951	8,915
1901	13,123

John Smiles Vickers was the inspector of nuisances in Beverley in East Yorkshire, as well as being an assistant overseer and a rate collector. In 1881 he gave evidence in the House of Lords on the Beverley Water Bill. He had previously given evidence on the same bill in the House of Commons.

Vickers was asked to comment on assertions by some people that, in Beverley, the top soil was saturated with sewage to a depth of 6 to 8ft.

While Vickers claimed to find this shocking, he went on to say that any back yard would get in that state if the people living there weren't clean, and any drain or cesspool might become choked up if it was not attended to. He also pointed out that the cesspools were all concreted and so were constantly damp. He hadn't seen one dry brick cesspool in the area. There were also around 2,000 ash pits in Beverley.

He referred to an incident in Lark Lane just the day before the hearing. He had gone to two adjoining homes and found the first had a back yard, which measured around 5 by 3yrds. Through the guttering, there was an open, uncovered ash pit and at the side of that and adjoining to the wall was a privy. This ash pit was three parts full of the detritus of the household, and the liquid parts were filtering through its wall and oozing into the soil on the ground. There was also a gully – or trap –close to the door, covered with rubbish and decaying vegetables.

The ash pits were built by brick and all above ground. They were also uncemented and constantly damp, due to the weather. Consequently, their contents could not be contained either.

Despite these filthy conditions, many of the local people resented the proposed bill to supply the town with waterworks, which would make it more sanitary. This is because, in these houses, the rates were paid by the tenants rather than their landlords and these would increase if the works went ahead. Vickers knew this, as he collected the rates himself and spoke to the tenants regularly.

He also said the people were not nearly so dirty as they had been described. He certainly hadn't witnessed persons living in offensive filth. If he had, he would have ordered the nuisance to be removed. The committee asked Vickers how he would get rid of such a nuisance if the tenants said they would not move it and he said he would serve them with a notice. This he had done on occasion – probably twice during the past year – for committing nuisances such as leaving manure in the streets.

Hartlepool 1883, Frederick Morris

The present system of drainage was 'bad, very bad, and very defective'.

Bill for extending the boundaries of the borough of Hartlepool and for other purposes.

Hartlepool population growth
1801	993
1851	9,503
1901	14,074

F.G. Morris was surveyor and inspector of nuisances for Hartlepool in County Durham. He gave evidence in the House of Commons on the Hartlepool Borough Extension Bill in 1883. He fulfilled the same position for the Throston Local Board and was responsible for the planned extensions proposed in the bill.

Morris was asked if the present system of drainage in Throston, a suburb of Hartlepool, was unquestionably bad. Morris described it as 'bad, very bad, and very defective'. Morris added that it was positively injurious, and said that if the bill was passed it would be the first issue attended to.

However, no plan had been agreed as to how the drainage would be dealt with. It had not even been considered by the Throston Local Board. Nevertheless, suggestions had been made by various people and Morris told the committee that there would be no engineering difficulty and no difficulty in disposing of the sewage of Throston properly. It was merely a question of expense, and the only choice was where the outfall was to be located.

Morris had been working in the district for thirty-two years. This was long enough to make himself acquainted with all the matters connected with Throston and he considered the sanitary arrangements to be very poor. If a combined scheme could be devised by which West Hartlepool could get rid of its sewage, that would save Throston as West Hartlepool would have to bear a proportion of the expense of the outfall. Morris thought a combined system would be better, and less expensive to Throston.

Morris told the committee there was a small, shifting population in the coastal district, as much of the population was engaged in shipping. A good deal of these people were from what he called the tramp class. He inspected their lodging houses to see that they conformed to the regulations and he was concerned that they were bringing diseases into the area. Even if a few people came into Throston with infectious diseases and were not properly attended to, the problem would spread and great swathes of Throston and West Hartlepool might suffer.

The committee quizzed Morris on whether there might be an advantage in merging the various districts in the Hartlepool area. He opposed any such merger, believing a reasonably sized district was better to manage than a larger one. He had not, however, advised his corporation not to agree to the districts joining.

Chapter 9

Rivers: Pollution and Blocked Dykes

Cardiff 1890, Thomas Williams

The river was black as ink.

Bill to authorise the sale and transfer of the Undertaking of the Bute Docks at Cardiff to the Taff Vale Railway Company; and for other purposes.

Cardiff population growth

1801	1,870
1851	18,351
1901	164,333

Thomas Williams was inspector of buildings to the Marquis of Bute, and gave evidence to the select committee on the Bute Docks at Cardiff Bill in 1890. He was well-acquainted with the valley of the Taff. Before taking service under the Marquis of Bute, he had been inspector of nuisances and surveyor of buildings to the Cardiff Rural Sanitary Authority for thirteen years. In that capacity, he had made a survey and report of the condition of the River Taff several times. The area he had covered had been from Cardiff to Merthyr, Aberdare and Treherbert.

In 1888, he received instructions to report on the condition of the River Taff at Merthyr. On each inspection, he had found great amounts of rubbish and filth had been deposited in the water. He also observed that scavenging refuse and sewage was going into the river at Merthyr. It was carried in great heaps from the houses and Williams knew it also went direct from the collieries. It was tipped into the river at the side and thrown into every opening in the river wall. On 9 January, he visited the Great Western Colliery and saw a large amount of refuse and ashes being thrown over the river wall into the water.

Williams told the committee that even when the rubbish was deposited on the riverbank, it was swept into the water. He was unsure whether the local authorities sanctioned this or not, but the town's refuse was there daily now. Williams had checked the day before the evidence session and all manner of rubbish was littering the bank.

Williams told the committee it was the same state of affairs at Pontypridd and Merthyr, where he witnessed scavengers and hauliers tipping rubbish into the river. At Treorchy, he saw employees of the local board taking a cart of refuse and road scrapings and dumping it in the river.

He knew that the authorities had fined some of their dust contractors for depositing rubbish on vacant spaces near the river, but it didn't prevent them from continuing to do it. On 26 and 27 January, there was a flood which carried away a large amount of debris from the valleys into the river. Williams thought this, combined with the general dumping of rubbish, was detrimental to the condition of the river.

Williams said it had been some three years since he had reported on the condition of the River Taff to Lord Bute. That had been in 1887, which was a very dry year, known as the 'great drought'. Williams would not speculate on whether some of the people who tipped cinders and other refuse into the river were Lord Bute's lessees.

The committee was not pleased by Williams' diffidence on this point, describing him as 'a most unusually cautious' man. The committee added that, as it assumed many of Lord Bute's tenants or lessees were offenders, it would be rather awkward if Bute had the power of picking and choosing who he would prosecute. Williams said he did not understand what that had to do with him at all. He said he was tired of their suppositions and told them all he could say was that he had seen rubbish dumped into the river.

Williams added that he knew the Pontypridd Local Board was endeavouring to prevent refuse being thrown into the stream in their district but it wasn't working. The committee said the Pontypridd Board were obviously doing their best to prevent the river from becoming contaminated but Williams tartly observed that if they did their best, they could stop it being done.

Williams was aware that the Pontypridd authorities published notices warning people not to offend against the Rivers Pollution Act 1876, and warning they would be prosecuted if they did. Williams told the committee that all the boards had their notices, but they were not carried out.

Williams agreed with the committee that the river was polluted by this solid stuff, because the river was black as ink. The committee probed Williams about fishing in the River Taff, but he cautioned that he was not a fisherman, and knew very little about fishing. However, he had never seen a man fishing twice in the river in his life.

Great Yarmouth 1907, Samuel Hassall

The chairman suggested that the whole area was a sort of Sodom and Gomorrah.

Bill to authorise the construction of further waterworks and the taking of water from the River Bure, for the purpose of affording increased supplies of water by the Great Yarmouth Water Works Company and the Lowestoft Water and Gas Company; to confer further powers upon those Companies with reference to their respective undertakings, and for other purposes.

Great Yarmouth population growth

1801	4,845
1951	26,880
1901	35,371

Samuel Hassall, the inspector of nuisances for the borough of Great Yarmouth, and an associate of the Royal Sanitary Institute, appeared before a select committee in 1907. The Great Yarmouth Waterworks and Lowestoft Water and Gas 1907 Bill were under discussion. He told the committee that in February 1906 he had made a careful examination of various points along the proposed point of water intake on the River Bure. He had been there again on subsequent occasions in 1907 with the medical officer of health of Great Yarmouth.

Hassall had with him a plan showing where the various places, which he was going to speak of, were situated. The committee pointed to Horning Ferry Inn, which was about two miles above the proposed point of water intake. Hassall explained that all of the inn, including the stables, cow sheds, pig sties and swill waste, discharged into a dyke, which ran at the back of the premises and went on for about 140yrds beside the roadway. It passed underneath a bridge and was pumped out by a windmill.

The dyke contained a great deal of filthy matter. The smell was objectionable and there were distinct traces of excrement, as a large pit half full of human faeces was nearby and a recent flooding caused it to be washed into the dyke. The occupier of the inn was dumping excrement in that pit.

The committee then questioned Hassall about the village of Horning Lower Street, a village of fifty to sixty houses. Hassall said there was no proper system of scavenging carried there and the occupants had to make what arrangements they could for the disposal of the house refuse. Nor was there a system of emptying their privies or pail closets of night soil. The committee thought they were all pail closets there, but Hassall said a good quantity of them had privies and some of them with privy middens were in close proximity to the water.

The people generally deposited the contents of their privies and privy middens on the land adjoining their premises, immediately beside the river. The road sloped down into the river, and there were a number of houses situated between the river and the roadway.

Hassall had tested the drains at The New Inn. He found the urinal and the swill water were connected with a 4-inch drain, which passed through two inspection chambers before being delivered into a boat house. This year the cutting where the boats were had been extended and it now went into the boat cutting direct, and thence directly into the river.

Hassell asked the inn owner what he did with refuse from the piggeries and the pail closets. He told Hassall 'we move it as occasion requires', but after rainfall a large amount of liquid filth drained into the river as there were no gullies to receive it. Even if there were, they would be connected to the river.

Hassall gave other examples, such as a row of cottages that threw their slops and liquid filth into the gully, which was situated in the roadway. When Hassall tested the roadway drains, he had found that the public sewer, as some people would call it, ran into the river. The committee chairman mused that these were all instances of people managing their household affairs within the provisions of the Public Health Act and there was no reason to change anything.

Hassall disagreed and said they were all nuisances, which could be removed if the law requiring this was strictly enforced, but it was difficult for even an active local authority to get rid of them in a rural district of this kind. Under the Rivers Pollution Act it was almost impossible to deal with such nuisances.

He pointed out that the insanitary conditions were having a detrimental effect on local tourism in the area, which brought a lot of money into the area. The Swan Hotel was a large hotel and holiday resort, which had provision for stabling for eight horses. It had three closets of the pedestal type and a couple of urinals, yet when Hassall recently inspected the hotel he found that the cesspool, which was not treated, was full up to the overflow, and there was a filthy turbid liquid running through the overflow, underneath the lawn, where the hotel's guests would sit in the summer. Waste from the Horseshoe Hotel also drained into the river. The Anchor Hotel had made some adjustments as a small cesspool had been built, which, although not lined, could be ladled out and put on the ground, whereas the year before it had been delivering right into the river.

The committee then questioned Hassall about the villages, Hope Town, St John and Wroxham, which were divided by the river and housed almost 1,000 people. In the summer the population swelled, as a great number of boathouses had been built which attracted visitors and tourists from all over the country.

Hassall said there was no general system of dealing with the sewage in this place whatsoever. Owners and occupiers had to make their own arrangements if they could, by paying for the emptying of their privies and pail closets. There was no scavenging. Many people just threw their waste into the river and the few drains he did find and tested flowed in there too. Some cesspools were only emptied once a year.

The whole of the public roadway drained into the river, which he said was filthy. The sediment from wheat-washing tanks caused the river to be foul. Hassall had dipped a boat oar in and found, on inspection, that there was a tremendous amount of sewage matter left on the oar.

The chairman suggested that the whole area was a sort of Sodom and Gomorrah and Hassall agreed. He said it applied to many streets, but often because the buildings were on a slope, leading towards the river.

Hassall contended that the various district councils ought to have made some kind of provision with regard to public sewers, but there had been no provision made – only those badly constructed sewers which connected right into the river.

The discussion then turned to Coltishall, a village which was home to around 1,000 people. The general system there, if it could be called a system, was not exactly the same, for the simple reason that one of the residents was a man named Gooch, who didn't do anything but empty privies, pail closets and cesspools. He was engaged by the residents to collect their night soil and so forth, which he did, and they paid him and he deposited the whole of the filth onto a meadow. Hassall and the medical officer had checked there a week before and found a great amount of human excrement and house refuse. When Hassall was there, he watched a man add a wheelbarrow's worth of refuse to the heap. It was obvious that, after heavy rainfall, the liquid would drain from this heap and enter the dyke, which went around this meadow, and deliver itself into the Bure. The whole of the meadow was a marsh and subject to flood.

Hassall said a real problem was that most of the owners of the properties, which were now polluting the River Bure, were members of either the district council or the respective parish councils, so that it was not likely that they were going to do very much unless they were forced to. Therefore, if the power was taken out of their hands and put in the hands of the water company, which had an interest in purifying the water, the problem could be resolved. Hassall said that if this didn't happen, the nuisance would continue as he was sure, from the information he had received in his enquiries over the past year, council members had no intention of spending any money with regards to the alteration of the drainage in their respective localities.

Hassall discussed with the committee whether he had enough powers to do his job effectively. The committee suggested that if he was the officer of a local authority under the Public Health Act he could do a great deal. Hassall said he could do more if he had the assistance of his authority. If the authority really was keen for alterations to be carried out, the nuisances could be done away with.

Chapter 10

Markets: Stinking Crabs and Ice Cream with Bugs

Ilford 1894, F. W. King

> *At the market, the good food was placed on the top, and the bad food was hidden below.*

Bill to authorise the Urban District Council of Ilford, in the county of Essex, to carry out street improvements; to make further provision for the improvement of health, local government, and finance of the district, and for other purposes.

Ilford population growth

1801	1,724
1851	3,742
1901	41,234

In 1894 a House of Commons committee, taking evidence on the Ilford Urban District Council Bill, heard evidence from F. W. King, the chief inspector of nuisances of Ilford in Essex.

King told the committee his attention had been drawn to the sale of unsound food. He had three or four cases a year with food from street hawkers a particular concern. The edible goods in question were almost always fish and apples.

King would ask to see the food before the hawkers took it to the market and, if it was unfit for public consumption, he would condemn it as unsound, seize and destroy it, and give the sellers a note to take back to the wholesale merchant. Sometimes they were compensated and sometimes they had difficulty getting anything for it.

If King passed the hawkers' food, it could be sold safely. However, occasionally, customers were short changed because at the market, the good food was placed on the top and the bad food was hidden below. King believed that, as so many hawkers were willing to sell inedible goods to people, if he didn't inspect as much as he did, there might be serious and wide-ranging consequences in the district.

Despite this, King could not give the committee any examples of a case where proceedings had been taken, and where it had been shown that the man who had the unsound food had bought it from the wholesale dealer, and that the wholesale dealer was really the person who ought to be prosecuted. King took it that the wholesale dealers admitted to selling bad food de facto by paying up for the loss of the goods King had seized.

East Ham 1898, Joseph Banks

Banks had a case, only a few days before, of a tub of crabs. The top ones were alive but two thirds of the barrel were stinking, dead crabs.

Bill to confer further powers upon the urban district council for East Ham in the county of Essex.

East Ham population growth
1901	1,165
1851	1,550
1901	96,008

NB East Ham was established as a county borough in 1878

Joseph Banks was inspector of nuisances in East Ham, London, and gave evidence in the House of Commons in 1898 on the East Ham Improvement Bill. He had held the position for three years and told the committee he was familiar with the conditions of trading in the small shops in East Ham.

Banks was concerned with his small traders buying unsound food, principally fish and fruit. They would buy what looked like good, fresh food from large markets but when they got home and undid the packaging, they would find the food beneath the top layer was rotten and could not be sold on. Very often they would bring the food round to Banks' office for him to see. Banks had a case only a few days before of a tub of crabs. The top ones were alive but two thirds of the barrel were stinking, dead crabs. Banks had no power to seize them but he gave the fishmonger a note to say they were unfit for human consumption and, with the fishmonger's agreement, Banks had the crabs destroyed. He hoped the new bill would give him the power to seize the contaminated food.

Banks was asked if he thought it was unfair to punish the small trader and instead focus on the larger vendor. Banks said the primary vendor should be reprimanded for palming off substandard goods but the smaller purchaser was at fault for not examining the goods he was exposing for sale, as he was not exercising sufficient care. Thus, he did not exempt the small vendor and in certain cases he wanted to punish them both.

Banks did, however, concede that it wasn't always practical to check all the food. For instance, supposing a man were to go up to Billingsgate Market and buy a dozen cases of fish, he wouldn't have the opportunity to examine all of them as he'd have to get back to his business. He might examine one or two, and those might be good, and instead of wasting his time examining the whole dozen he would take these two as a sample.

Yet Banks also believed that if the food was only half bad, some traders would take a chance and sell it on and so the practice had to be stopped once and for all, with prosecution.

Banks said that what he was proposing was an amendment of the law. The committee suggested he was proposing to make a crime in East Ham something that was not a crime in other parts of the country. However, Banks said that by amending the law, it would benefit the small vendors in the long term.

Presently, a small trader might be summoned before a magistrate and fined, even if it had not been his fault. However, the public did not take this into account. They ceased dealing with him because he had been convicted of selling articles unfit for human food. The small trader could lose his livelihood. He could receive financial compensation but he could not recover the loss and damage of his reputation. Meanwhile, the original vendor could get off scot-free.

Banks suggested both sellers should be brought before the magistrates and he would see them both together. The public would then see from the decision that the vendor had himself been deceived. Yes, the small trader had not exercised the proper amount of care but it would be obvious if he was the unwitting and unwary instrument of fraud.

The powers Banks was seeking for East Ham had already existed for the past five years in neighbouring West Ham. Banks believed they had worked very well there. He was familiar with their effects as, for two years, he had been inspector of nuisances in West Ham. Banks recalled a case of a shopkeeper selling unsound condensed milk. The council decided to prosecute the wholesale dealer, not the shopkeeper. It was appealed against in the lower court but the council won, as did the small trader in the eyes of the public.

Banks told the committee he did sometimes catch these wholesale dealers supplying hawkers with unsound fruit. At the end of the market, when all the shopkeepers had got their supplies, the leftovers were sold to the costermongers (someone selling fruit and vegetables from a barrow), to hawkers and to the crowds in the East End and Banks could keep an eye out and intercept if the food sold on was not edible. There had been a case when grapes taken from the gutter were sold to a costermonger and Banks' men seized them. The costermonger was prosecuted and he went to prison for a short time, and they proceeded against the wholesale man as well, and he was convicted.

The committee told Banks it was not seeking to make this a criminal offence, but, as such powers had been taken in West Ham in 1893, it was odd that an act in West Ham could be considered criminal while 2yrds away over the border the same offence faced no redress. Banks asked that those powers should be applied to East Ham for the protection of those persons who purchased goods from small traders, and for the protection of the small traders themselves.

Banks explained that the boundary between East and West Ham was the great central market for the two districts, and on one side they had these powers, and on the other they did not. It was a large market: thousands of people assembled there every Saturday and costermongers came from all parts of London.

Banks said that if he had seized fish in West Ham that had been sold in Billingsgate he could go to Billingsgate and prosecute the original vendor. He couldn't, however, do the same if the fish was bought in East Ham.

The chairman observed that the clause Banks was seeking would only empower him to prosecute the original vendor if he lived in the East

Ham district. Banks disagreed and said as long as the food was sold in East Ham, he could prosecute the wholesale vendor wherever he was in the country. He pointed out that there had been a case in the paper just the day before of a man fined for supplying diseased meat in Lincoln to a London market. However, both Banks and the committee agreed that this section of the bill was fraught with many difficulties of interpretation.

Leicester 1908, William Tyldesley

There were a number of men who dealt in a very poor class of animal, which was emaciated and unfit to be slaughtered for food.

Bill to extend the limits for the supply of gas and water by the Mayor, Aldermen and Burgesses of the County Borough of Leicester, and to confer further powers with respect to electricity, milk supply and streets and buildings, and to make further provision with respect to sanitary matters and for the good government of the Borough and for other purposes.

Leicester population growth

1801	17,905
1851	65,405
1901	211,579

William Tyldesley was meat inspector and inspector of nuisances in Leicester. He gave evidence in the House of Commons in 1908 on the Leicester Corporation Bill.

He told the committee that, as Leicester was an agricultural centre, a large cattle market was held there every Wednesday. It was his business to attend the market to inspect the animals and also to inspect the slaughterhouses, of which there were seventy in the borough.

It was also his duty to inspect butchers' shops and fishmongers for the purpose of enforcing the unsound meat clauses of the Public Health Act. Tyldesley believed there were a number of men who dealt in a very poor class of animal, which was emaciated and unfit to be slaughtered for food. However, these men attended the country market with the sole purpose of selling these animals on.

Tyldesley had seized animals several times in the course of his duty, as well as rotten meat. He was under no illusion that the owners knew both were unfit for human consumption but they still attempted to sell them to local shopkeepers. In fact, in Tyldesley's experience, these men would do their utmost to get hold of poor meat at a cheap price. They would often sell it to numerous small retailers. Recently, he had found part of the carcass of an unfit beast distributed in three different places.

Under the current practices, Tyldesley could only deal with the shopkeepers in his district and was powerless to prevent the wholesale traders from outside the area coming to the market and selling diseased animals or bad meat to them. He knew that unless a bill was passed, he would never be able to get at the root of this evil and protect his residents from eating potentially dangerous food.

Tyldesley also pointed out that in a large town like Leicester, the job of inspector was too much work for one man. He believed that in order to eliminate this problem once and for all and to be able to inspect markets, slaughterhouses, butchers and shops on a regular basis, two, three or even four inspectors should be appointed.

Bradford 1913, Frank White

He had found ice cream stored in stables and covered with filthy sacking smeared with horse dung.

Bill to confer powers on the Lord Mayor, Aldermen and citizens of the city of Bradford for the construction of waterworks, street works and improvements and the acquisition of lands, for the provision of trolley vehicles, with respect to infectious diseases, and the health, good government and sanitation of the city, to authorise the establishment of superannuation and other funds and to make provisions with respect to various matters of local administration and management.

Bradford population growth
1801	6,000
1841	108,000
1901	279,000

Frank White was the superintendent and chief inspector of nuisances in Bradford, Yorkshire in 1913. He was responsible for the area's ice-cream sellers and they caused him a lot of trouble.

He had found that ice cream in Bradford was produced in filthy and disgusting conditions. He had found ice cream stored in stables and covered with filthy sacking smeared with horse dung. He had found ice cream stored in bedrooms, which were occupied by nine people. He had found ice cream in pails in freezers covered with bugs, and when he brought this to the attention of the Italian ice-cream seller, he simply killed the bugs by crushing them against the side of the freezer so they fell into the ice cream. White's officers had also found ice cream stored in filthy cellars with defective drains.

In the past nine years, White had convicted many vendors, nineteen of whom received the maximum penalty. Nevertheless, the problem persisted with eleven cases in the past two years. The same people were being penalized. The ice-cream sellers would pay the fine again and again, and White thought they treated the punishment like a huge joke. After paying the penalty, some even turned round and laughed at him as they walked out of court. White thought it was essential that in the interests of the public, the fine should be increased considerably as it wasn't working as a deterrent.

White had worked as inspector of nuisance in Halifax and Sheffield but could honestly say that he had never seen conditions as disgusting as those he found in Bradford.

Chapter 11

The Slaughter of Animals

Birmingham 1861, James Bliss

> *Bliss had seen a heap of manure in the summertime undulating like waves –backwards and forwards – from the maggots moving inside.*

This is further evidence of the same 1861 bill featured in chapter 2.

Birmingham population growth

1801	84,711
1851	232,538
1901	522,204

In 1861, Birmingham's inspector of nuisances, James Bliss, gave evidence to a parliamentary select committee for the third time — on this occasion in the House of Lords — on the Birmingham Improvement Bill. He told the committee he had been an inspector for fifteen years.

His evidence centered on the building of slaughterhouses in populous districts of the borough; a process he thought was ill-advised. While he said some were offensive, when pushed he added that he did not think they were injurious to health (although he acknowledged that he had no medical training on which to judge this).

He explained that pigs were kept in most of the slaughterhouses and these pigs were fed offal. This was thrown to them in an unclean state and while they would eat some of it, any leftovers were thrown into a manure pit.

This animal matter would get mixed with the manure and it would begin to ferment. The stench was so bad that when one of the pits was emptied, the whole neighbourhood had to be fumigated for days. Bliss had seen a heap of manure in the summertime undulating like waves – backwards and forwards – from the maggots moving inside. He had insisted that lime was thrown on to destroy the insects.

The heap would grow for a long time until it weighed four or five tons, and only then was it carried away. The process of carrying it away was also very offensive to the neighbourhood and Bliss had received a number of complaints about this. However, he currently had no power to intervene and could only ask the butcher to put some lime in the heap to destroy the maggots and the smell.

Bliss told the committee there were 350 registered and licensed butchers and slaughterhouses in the borough. Some, not all, killed cattle. Generally, they were scattered over the whole town but there was a concentration of twenty-three at the back of the Shambles.

There had been many complaints about the slaughterhouses but the complainants did not like to have their names mentioned because they derived their living from gentlemen who owned these slaughterhouses. They complained to Bliss but begged that he did not mention their names.

Bliss said that he tried to ensure that the slaughterhouses were kept as clean as possible and only had to summon the owners to court ten or twelve times a year. As most of the slaughterhouses were scattered around town, Bliss and his assistants needed three or four horses to get to them and not all could be visited as often as he would like. However, he had strict rules that had to be adhered to.

First, every owner had to ensure their slaughterhouse was well-ventilated and thoroughly whitewashed with quicklime, at least twice a year.

A sufficient number of tubs, boxes or vessels with tight, close-fitting covers had to be built, to the satisfaction of the council, for the purposes of receiving and conveying all manure, garbage and filth immediately after the killing and dressing of any cattle. These were then removed beyond the limits of the borough, or to a place designated by the council. This was to happen at least once a day between 10pm and 8am.

All the blood from the slaughtering of cattle was to be put into separate tubs or vessels with close-fitting covers and carried away from the slaughterhouse without delay. It was not permitted to flow in the channel, sewer or open street. No blood was to be mixed with the manure, garbage or other filth. After use, all these tubs or vessels were to be cleaned thoroughly.

The carcasses and skins of animals were to be removed from the slaughterhouse within two days of cattle having been slaughtered. No cattle were to be kept in the slaughterhouse for more than three days before being slaughtered. The occupiers of slaughterhouses were not able to keep ferocious dogs in the premises unless the dogs were securely fastened or muzzled.

If an occupier of any slaughterhouse within the borough failed to comply with any of these bye-laws, failed to clean or whitewash the slaughterhouse after due notice from the council, or refused to allow any member, officer or servant of the council an inspection of the premises, he would pay for each and every offence a sum not exceeding £5. There would be a further cumulative penalty of ten shillings during the continuation of the offence after written notice from the council.

The bye-laws made various stipulations regarding the recovery of penalties imposed under them.

Currently Bliss only had power to remove slaughterhouses or to discontinue them if they became unoccupied. The committee asked Bliss if he thought the land for new slaughterhouses should be purchased at some distance from the borough. He said he didn't think the distance mattered as long as they were all close to each other, as then they could be supervised easily and more thoroughly. However, he said the council had never asked him his opinion about this.

He added that even if new slaughterhouses were built, he couldn't see the ones in the town being given up, as the owners would want to hold on to them for as long as they could. The committee asked Bliss if he thought the current slaughterhouses were big enough to accommodate the butchers. He said it depended, some were and some weren't. Some were small private family butchers while others were large carcass butchers.

Bliss knew all the butchers in Birmingham, many of whom (but not all) he said were gentlemen who wanted to have the bye-laws carried out. The committee then asked Bliss if it was true that butchers were, by and large, healthy people. He replied that they looked healthy and their wives looked healthy and were particularly buxom. However, he warned the committee that they should not take everyone by their looks as whenever the butchers became unwell they would very quickly 'go off'. Bliss had noticed that they would get saturated with the smell from the slaughterhouses, and those that were seriously ill did not last long before they died.

Leeds 1870, William Swale

The condemned meat made the pigs large in size and Swale would not have liked to have eaten them.

Bill for empowering the Mayor, Aldermen and Burgesses of the Borough of Leeds to erect gas works and supply gas within the parish and borough of Leeds, and township of Roundhay in the parish of Barwick-in-Elmet, all in the West Riding of the County of York, and for making further provision with respect to the sanitary condition of the Borough of Leeds, the providing of slaughterhouses and for other purposes.

Leeds population growth

1801	53,162
1851	101,343
1901	428,968

William Swale was a superintendent inspector of nuisances of works for cleaning and watering the streets of Leeds. He was also responsible for enforcing the law regarding slaughterhouses. Under the Leeds Improvement Act 1856 further powers were given to the corporation, including the power to make bye-laws. Under those bye-laws, it was Swale's duty to take proceedings against all offenders.

When he gave evidence in 1870, Swale was asked what response he got when he attempted to put the bye-laws into force. He said he was invariably met by strong opposition, which involved a vast deal of litigation and trouble, and was abortive in its results.

He named a Messrs Watson which had been particularly difficult. Swale had summoned and fined the owner for having an opening from his slaughterhouse into his shop. The law stated that there should be no opening and the thickness of the wall dividing animals being butchered and the area where meat was for sale should be sufficient. Swale told the committee that eventually he'd managed to prosecute him for 'disobedience'.

However, by and large, the bye-laws were unworkable, unenforceable and the slaughterhouse owners knew how to work around them. The authorities were also remiss in carrying them out.

Swale was glad to say he had not seen any local slaughterhouses (or, in the words of one committee member, 'dens of iniquity') during the last two years as he had left Leeds to work in London. However, from his earlier experience, the process of providing meat for the residents was highly objectionable. Prior to the Leeds Improvement Act in 1856, cattle were slaughtered in the open streets. Only since then had slaughterhouses been built, and now there were many of them.

Swale was asked whether it was possible to inspect all the slaughterhouses thoroughly. He responded by saying the job was so big it could only be done if each slaughterhouse had two inspectors, as someone would need to be there day and night and one man could not do that. Without that type of constant, close inspection, any diseased meat would simply be sold on by the owners who were only too happy to dupe the public into buying rotten food.

Swale believed that if each district had one central slaughterhouse which was under the corporation's control, it would be more satisfactory to the butchers and small traders who were being fobbed off with meat unfit for public consumption.

He was aware of many bad practices and the owners worked together to prevent Swale and his colleagues from doing their job. They did this by 'flying bad meat'. This meant that if Swale was inspecting slaughterhouse number twelve, number sixteen, knowing he was on his rounds and due to visit, would take an animal and have the innards – lungs, liver and offal; all of the parts that indicated its good health or diseased state – taken or 'flown' away. Swale had known of such cases and with six slaughterhouses scattered all over the borough, it was difficult for him to keep an eye on them all. Having them concentrated in one area, on corporation-owned land, close to each other but no more than two miles from the butchers, would be beneficial as they could be supervised and practices would be improved.

Swale could not tell the committee the percentage of meat that was diseased when brought into the borough, although from memory he thought it was a very large percentage. To give a sense of scale, Swale estimated that 3,000 to 5,000 animals, including sheep, were killed each year in Leeds, and if he examined 300 or 400 a month, eighty to 100 beasts, or around thirty to forty per cent, were partly diseased and would be condemned. The rest would be passed for consumption.

However, Swale did not think that the quantity of condemned meat was a true indicator of the quantity of bad meat. He believed a fair amount of rotten meat was being knowingly sold on as food for humans.

A good deal of the diseased meat did go to feed pigs but he didn't approve of that either. Swale thought it was an objectionable way of disposing of it. The committee observed that the pigs who were fed condemned meat were surely diseased themselves and Swale agreed. He said the condemned meat made the pigs large in size and Swale would not have liked to have eaten them. However, he also said he'd seen many pigs who weren't eating the bad meat and were still full of disease. Often these pigs would end up on the dinner plate.

Swale was then asked to turn his attention to the bodies and skins of animals which were also sold. He said the large amount of bad meat in the borough meant anyone with the right money had as much chance of getting a bad carcass as they did a good one.

The magistrates did have the power to prosecute corrupt slaughterhouse owners and have the meat destroyed, but this happened in fewer than one per cent of cases. Swale thought this was remiss as it meant the nuisance simply continued.

Darwen 1887, William Armitage

People kept so much poultry that the yards were very dirty. There had been complaints from people who said fearful smells were coming into their back yards from their neighbours who kept poultry and pigeons.

Bill to alter the names of the Borough and of the Corporation of Over Darwen to extend the limits of gas supply of the Corporation, and to confer upon them further powers in relation to their water and gas undertaking to make further provision for the improvement and good government of the Borough.

Darwen population growth
1801	25,233
1851	77,270
1901	76,140

William Armitage was the inspector of nuisances of Over Darwen in Lancashire and gave evidence in the House of Commons in 1887 on the Over Darwen Corporation (Police and Sanitary Regulations) Bill. He told the committee he was a medical man.

Armitage said people kept so much poultry that their yards were very dirty. There had been complaints from people who said objectionable smells were coming into their back yards from their neighbours who kept poultry and pigeons.

The committee wondered whether anyone who was aggrieved by these smells made a report to the medical officer of health, as the medical officer had the power to direct the removal of the nuisance. Armitage replied that they did and the medical officer would report to the council. Then, if the appropriate committee thought it was worth taking action, the offending houses would be served with notices ordering them to remove the birds. If the medical officer of health was prepared to support the case with evidence, then the council would proceed.

Armitage acknowledged that there was difficulty in obtaining evidence. For example, the council didn't consider keeping pigeons for the sport of flying was a nuisance, even if the medical officer and inspector disagreed.

Armitage admitted he did not know of any cases of disease caused by the birds. He had never taken out summonses against people but he had served them with notices. In most cases, this solved the problem for a little while but it was only a matter of time before they began to keep birds again.

Blackburn 1888, George Lewis

A dead horse was not as bad to look at as it was to smell.

Bill to authorise the Corporation of the county borough of Blackburn to acquire the undertaking of the Blackburn Corporation Tramways Company Limited and to construct new tramways in the borough; to improve and work the undertaking; to partially consolidate the redeemable debt and mortgages of the Corporation; to consolidate and apply sinking funds; to repeal borrowing powers; to borrow money, and for other purposes.

Blackburn population growth

1801	11,980
1851	46,536
1901	129,216

Isaac George Lewis was inspector of nuisances in Blackburn in Lancashire and gave evidence in the House of Commons on the Blackburn Corporation Tramways Bill in 1888. He told the committee that animal carcasses were being carried through the streets of the borough day and night. He had observed this over the past two weeks and, from what he saw, had calculated that this was not an occasional event but it was happening 2,106 times a year.

The problem was at its worst in Blackburn due to its location. Animals from Preston, Burnley and large rural districts were being brought into the town and carried through it. Some of these had travelled long distances and, as the roads they were travelling on were poor and uneven, the cover shielding the bodies from the public was in disarray by the time it reached Blackburn. Often, the legs and the heads of the animals were on full view, and blood could be seen oozing from the beasts as they were bumped along the ground in carts.

A committee member commented that surely the sight of the bloodied animal was not as bad as the odour and added that a dead horse was not as bad to look at as it was to smell. There was some truth in that as a great many carcasses were in a putrid condition and the stench was obnoxious. Only the day before the session, Lewis had received a complaint about two cows that were being carted through the streets of Blackburn, which smelt very bad.

In view of this, Lewis was asking for power to prevent such an event happening in daytime when the streets were full of people. He proposed that 'it shall not be lawful for any person to convey or cause to be conveyed through the streets of the borough carcasses between the hours of 8am and 8pm.'

Lewis thought that this curfew would not cause any serious disturbance to the trade and, as the animals came from a distance, it would be easy to time their arrival at night. They could also travel a similar route as the majority were going to the same place. During the fortnight that he'd been carrying out his surveillance, seventy-four were taken to a place just outside the borough, but had to pass through the town to reach it. Only seven were removed to a knacker's yard within the borough.

The committee discussed whether the Municipal Corporations Act gave Lewis power to frame an appropriate bye-law. However, one member observed that no bye-law could meet the need Lewis was raising to prohibit the carriage of carcasses between certain hours, unless it identified that each carcass was a nuisance. Lewis said he did not want to have to treat each case individually and prove each carcass was a nuisance. As a large number of these animals were being brought in, general powers were needed to regulate this.

Chapter 12

Diseases

Halifax 1853, Samuel Magson

Cattle were left to stand on the streets, and Magson received complaints from residents who were becoming ill.

Bill for the Improvement of the Borough of Halifax.

Halifax population growth
1801 (township)	8,886
1851 (borough)	22,582
1901 (borough)	104,936

Samuel Magson was inspector of nuisances in Halifax, Yorkshire, and gave evidence in the House of Commons in 1853 on the Halifax Waterworks and Improvement (Halifax Waterworks and Extension) Bill in 1853. He had been attached to the police force in one capacity or another since its commencement in 1848 and became inspector of nuisances in 1851.

Magson was concerned with the lack of water in the borough. The present water supply – the waterworks – only extended to a part of Halifax and water was only available two or three times a week and sometimes the flow was feeble. Magson also told the committee that some residents were being charged one pound three pence a day for water for three days. The committee was shocked and asked what the payment was for and he said it was for it to be fetched in cans by galloways (small horses) and donkeys. Magson told the disbelieving committee these people – who were middle class and had taps in their kitchens – had to pay this despite, allegedly, already paying rates for a water supply.

However, Halifax residents were relatively lucky as adjacent townships of Northowram and Southowram and several other localities, such as Mount Pellon, Kings Cross, Trafalgar and Wyke, had no water supply at all. These areas were also populous but were occupied chiefly by people of the poorer classes whom Magson described as 'cottagers'. They had to rely on pumps and wells for water and suffered greatly, especially in the summer, when these would run dry.

The lack of a substantial, wholesome water supply meant that the district was riddled with sickness and disease. A private reservoir at the top of Range Bank supplied some houses but it was so bad that some people had their taps cut off on account of the water's impurity. During the summer, there was also a considerable stench as drains or sewers ran into Hebble Brook, which became horribly contaminated. There simply wasn't enough water to flush the brook.

People were also becoming ill due to the way animals for slaughter were being kept. Cattle markets were held in the thoroughfares and cattle were left to stand on the streets, and Magson received complaints from residents who were becoming ill. The committee proposed a new market site, which Magson supported as it was on an incline and was capable of being effectively drained.

The slaughterhouses were also in a sorry state. They were concentrated in the centre of a closely populated part of Halifax and Magson found sickness was prevalent in these neighbourhoods as there wasn't enough water to keep them clean and this led to poor-quality meat finding its way on to the dinner plate.

Bury 1885, William Porritt

Two young persons, both of whom had been afflicted with scarlet fever during infancy, were struck down with diphtheria and one died.

Bill to extend the Municipal Boundary of the Borough of Bury; to confer further powers upon the Corporation of Bury with respect to their Gas and Winter Undertaking; and to make further provision for the good government of the Borough; to authorise the Creation of Corporation Stock.

Bury population growth

1801	7,072
1851	25,484
1901	123,832

Having given evidence on the Bury Improvement Bill in the House of Commons, William Porritt, Bury's inspector of nuisances gave evidence on the same bill before a committee in the House of Lords. His area of responsibility extended over the whole of the sanitary authority, comprising ten townships.

Porritt worked closely with a medical officer called Dr Bank who took a great interest in sanitary matters. Porritt said that he and Bank (who was not in attendance) published an annual report, which he produced for the committee to read. It recorded eighteen deaths due to scarlet fever.

There had been an epidemic of scarlet fever in and around the village of Summerseat in the spring. A family at Wood Road and another at Higher Summerseat each lost two children from a malignant type of the disease. At nearby Pigslee, the summer saw an outbreak which affected eight children, three of whom died. At the same time, two young persons, both of whom had been afflicted with scarlet fever during infancy, were struck down with diphtheria and one died.

On inspecting the block of dwellings where the children lived, Porritt found the back premises were in a disgraceful condition. The subsoil was saturated with liquid filth from an open cesspool and several pig sties which, at the time of inspection, flowed towards the cottages. The old drains, which ran directly under the floors of the rooms in which they lived, were blocked with decomposing organic filth, and particles from this were being circulated into the rooms by the untapped slop stone pipes. Porritt also learned that the eighteen pigs who were kept there had been suffering from a disease people called the 'reds'.

Porritt said he took immediate steps to correct this shocking state of affairs. The old drains were removed and new drains were installed outside the houses. The slop stone pipes were disconnected from the new drains, the pigs were removed, and the houses where fever had existed were thoroughly cleansed and disinfected.

This outbreak was, said Porritt, interesting in that it threw some light upon the relationship between scarlet fever and diphtheria occurring, as this epidemic did, immediately after hot, dry weather in the immediate vicinity of foul emanations from unclean drains.

Porritt drew the committee's attention to the typhoid epidemic that was listed in the report and which occurred the year before. He thought typhoid fever could be connected with defective sanitary arrangements as, in March 1884, a serious outbreak of this disease had occurred at Tottington. The Rural Sanitary Authority had a sewer running through Tottington and the water in the brooks, streams and the River Irwell was discoloured and polluted as refuse from local factories was draining into it. Porritt insisted, however, that no domestic sewage was getting into the water and when the committee said it had been told that the sides of the brooks smelt badly owing to the sewage matter from houses that had been deposited on the sides, Porritt claimed he had never smelt them. The committee asked Porritt if he had the facility for smelling a disagreeable smell and he reassured them that he had a very good sense of smell.

The committee referred to a sample of water that had been produced. It said it clearly showed the stream was polluted but Porritt added he did not think it a fair sample of the water sent down from the Whiteheads Works. Porritt pointed his finger squarely at the factories but admitted that he didn't know how to alter their behaviour without damaging trade. He added that manufacturers dumping refuse in rivers was a nuisance throughout Lancashire. However, he said he was pleased with the steps the authority was taking to raise the standards of hygiene and this had been reflected in the fact typhoid no longer affected the area. There had been one case of smallpox some three or four years before when smallpox was raging in Bury and the neighbouring districts, but that had not returned.

The committee then turned to consider three cottages near a place called Botholt. They had been told the excreta there ran from the water closets into the garden by means of a pipe cut into the ground, which then led into the brook. Porritt said he had not seen it. He had passed the houses many times but had never inspected them so he could not confirm if this was true.

They asked him to consider an area called Anthony Fields where they believed the ash pits were simply holes. Porritt said there might be one or two ash pits there but not too many and not many of the houses had imperfect sanitary arrangements.

The committee was not pleased and pointed to a report signed by him in 1883, which said that, in the absence of any organized scheme for removing night soil, a number of privy nuisances had arisen, which had to be dealt with individually and repeatedly, 'but as the more thickly populated portions of the district became absorbed into urban centres, this difficulty would disappear.' The committee said it was obviously still a problem but Porritt disagreed.

The committee asked Porritt if there were worse places in Bury than the ones under his jurisdiction. He said that although he had been criticized, he would not like to criticize another authority as he was not one to meddle.

Guildford 1886, Thomas Rees

> *He would make thorough enquiries into the situation and report on the condition of the patients, whether they had a bad case of smallpox or a bad case of fever.*

Bill to extend the boundaries of the Borough of Guildford, to confer further powers upon the Corporation of Guildford with respect to their water undertaking, to make further provision for the good government of the Borough, to authorise the creation of Corporation stock and for other purposes.

Guildford population growth

Year	Population
1801	11,992
1851	20,940
1901	43,118

Thomas Rees was the inspector of nuisances for the Guildford Sanitary Authority, and gave evidence in the House of Commons in 1886 on the Guildford Corporation (Police and Sanitary Regulations) Bill.

The committee told Rees it had been suggested that the medical officer of health for the district had not been making reports on people that were removed to the isolation hospital due to infectious disease. Rees said cases of that kind were reported through the inspector of nuisances. When he received notice of a case, he would make thorough enquiries into the situation and report on the condition of the patients, whether they had a bad case of smallpox or a bad case of fever. A letter was then sent, by post, to the medical officer, who, as a rule, would come down by the first train and visit the patients in the morning. The medical officer, added Rees, was also the borough coroner.

Guildford had no isolation hospital. Rees believed that the late Lord Onslow had donated a site for one to be built but the Corporation of Guildford had never done anything about it. When questioned about this, the corporation told the committee that even though it didn't have much experience of dealing with infectious diseases, it was building its own isolation hospital. Rees dismissed the building they were referring to, which was currently used for disinfecting articles of clothing. He said it was ancient in style and appearance and was nothing more than a wooden shed. It would certainly not make an isolation hospital.

Clacton 1905, Arthur Shaddick

He'd had babies of under a year old whose parents would not pay for treatment. What could he do? Leave them to die?

Bill to confer further powers on the Urban District Council of Clacton in regard to the seashore recreation ground and other matters, and to make further and better provisions in regard to the health, local government and improvement of their district, and for other purposes.

Clacton population growth

1801	904
1851	1,281
1901	3,384

Arthur Shaddick was the inspector of nuisances for Clacton Urban District Council in London. He was the only witness to give evidence in a House of Commons select committee on the Clacton Improvement Bill in 1905.

Shaddick was asked how many earth closets needed to be converted into water closets and he said about fifty. He said the water supply in Clacton was abundant and the sewage arrangements were satisfactory, with two places of discharge – one to the east, and one to the west of the town.

The committee went on to consider Clause 57, which was notice of intention to repair drains. Shaddick was asked why he wanted that clause included and he said because, in his role as inspector of nuisances, he had uncovered many drains which had been 'repaired in order to clear a blockage'. In these cases, a hole would be made in the pipe, rods would be put down to get rid of the obstruction and something flimsy would be placed over the hole, such as a piece of tin or Catesby's lino. (Edward Catesby opened a carpet and lino shop in Marylebone in 1865 and moved to Tottenham Court Road in 1885: his lino shop was referred to in James Joyce's *Ulysses.)*

Shaddick believed introducing the clause would compel people to repair the drains properly. He said that on occasion, when called to a house in which the residents had been struck down with an infectious disease, he would find a drain that had been fixed in this way. He believed the appalling DIY was putting people at risk.

Despite this, the committee chairman announced that Clacton did not require legislation that the rest of the country didn't have and Clause 57 was struck out.

Attention was then turned to Clause 73 of the bill, which related to disinfection and 'filthy and dangerous articles to be putrefied'. The committee asked to speak to Clacton's medical officer, but was told he was very ill. However, Shaddick said he knew as much as the medical officer about sanitary issues and he could answer the questions.

The committee asked Shaddick if the council had an efficient system for disinfecting vehicles and houses. Shaddick replied that it did: it used a Thresher steam disinfector to disinfect the inside of vehicles and an alformant lamp (a special lamp which used formalin to fumigate bedding and furniture) as well as formalin spray. Bedding and clothing were carried from houses in a brougham (horse-drawn ambulance). Shaddick personally superintended all of that himself, even though he worked full time. He then said his medical officer did not give all his time to Clacton Council, and that when he needed assistance in the way of 'rough work', he got it from one of the women of the yard.

Clause 73 was passed and the committee discussed Clause 79: 'Power to medical officer to examine school children' and Clause 84: 'Expense of patients in hospitals'.

The committee asked Shaddick if most of his hospitals were occupied by children who belonged, not to locals, but to visitors. He replied that they were. This meant that if the parents refused to pay the medical costs incurred by caring for their children, there was nothing he could do. This was because current laws said the council shall recover all costs from the patient and as the patient was a minor, the council couldn't proceed against them. Nearly all parents had used this to their benefit and said they shouldn't pay as they weren't the patients. It was rare that he would get the full amount paid even though he said his charges were moderate. At present, the expense of maintaining Clacton's visitors' children was being picked up by the ratepayer.

The problem was that if a child with an infectious disease was brought to hospital, delaying treatment to give Shaddick enough time to locate the parents and get them to sign an agreement could mean the disease would spread to other patients. It was far too risky. He'd had babies of under a year old whose parents would not pay for treatment. What could he do? Leave them to die?

Shaddick thought it was Clacton's duty to get infectious cases into the hospital and seen to at once. But he also thought he should be able to recover the expense of taking immediate action and saving the child from greater illness or even death. The cost for each young patient was relatively small, but when there was a number of children it was a serious burden on Clacton's ratepayers.

Mynyddislwyn 1913, James Brown

Rag-and-bone men would carry sweets loose in a box, handle the rags and then give the treats out to children. The carts were filthy, as were the men.

Bill to empower the Urban District Council of Mynyddislwyn to purchase the gas undertakings and to supply gas within the Sirhowy Valley portion of their district; to make further provision in regard to the improvement and local government of the district, and for other purposes.

Mynyddislwyn population growth

1801	2,782
1851	9,076
1901	18,024

James Brown was inspector of nuisances and building inspector to Mynyddislwyn Council. He gave evidence in 1913 in the House of Commons on the Mynyddislwyn Urban District Council Bill.

Brown told the committee he was an associate member of the Royal Sanitary Institute, a member of the Royal College of Surgeons and licentiate of the Royal College of Physicians. He was also medical officer of health to the Mynyddislwyn District Council and the adjoining urban district of Abercarn.

Brown said it was a common practice for the rag-and-bone dealers in his district to carry oranges or sweets, and give them out in exchange for rags. The men would carry sweets loose in a box, handle the rags and then give the treats out to children. The carts were filthy, as were the men. He observed them rooting around in tips and handling all manner of refuse. They carried old bags of rubbish and little children would run to meet them excitedly, carrying rags. The week before he had seen a cart carrying oranges, which were prevented from rolling about by a number of filthy old bones. He conceded that there was an outside skin on the oranges that kept them protected but said that sometimes the children would eat the peel.

He said a medical man had told him that an outbreak of sores in the mouths of local children had been caused by these dirty and unhealthy practices.

Brown was asked if there was any bye-law regarding this, and he observed that the Home Office told him there was no power to make a bye-law but that 'the committee might enquire what special need for any provision to this effect had been experienced at Mynyddislwyn.' It was a new point, and had never been raised in front of the select committee before.

Brown said that in some districts, rag-and-bone men gave out toys or balloons instead of fruit and sweets and this was far less dangerous and unhealthy. In Lancashire they gave stones, which were used for rubbing on the flags. He urged the committee to introduce a clause in the bill that prevented these men from rewarding the children of Mynyddislwyn with edible treats.

Chapter 13

Industrialization

Manchester 1856, James Fox

> *If he saw a chimney smoking he would walk straight in to the building and tell the people that it wasn't allowed.*

Bill to amend an Act passed in the seventh and eighth years of his late Majesty King George IV, Bill to alter, amend, and enlarge the Powers and Provisions of an Act relating to the Road from Barnsdale through Pontefract to Thwaite Gate near Leeds in the West Riding of the County of York, and to continue the term thereby granted.

Manchester population growth

1801	70,409
1851	86,986
1901	543,372

James Fox was a superintendent of Manchester Corporation's nuisance department, and gave evidence in the House of Lords in 1856 on the Leeds Improvement Acts (Amendment) Bill. He had previously been the smoke inspector for the corporation and had a good many cases applied to the consumption of smoke and the raising of chimneys.

Fox told the committee there were dyers of various descriptions in Manchester. In many cases, where the smoke came from pans, it went into the same chimney as the smoke from the engine furnaces. Previous legislation had insisted chimneys should be raised to a height of at least 90ft. However, this wasn't always adhered to and Fox had issued around sixty notices to parties in different trades, works, manufacturers and workshops.

After Fox served a notice, the Nuisance Committee's sub-committee would meet and consider any complaints made, such as the case of Bowler's Works, a large maker of wheels for locomotives.

Bowler had a tall chimney, into which smoke from a furnace (which heated ties for wheels) would go. Bowler required a great deal of heat and the smoke was so great that Fox had to intervene and he served a notice. However, Bowler said it was impossible to reduce the smoke.

Fox was instructed by the town clerk to prove that it could be reduced, and to do that he obtained evidence from a Mr W. Forsyth, who said it was certainly possible and thus Bowler was convicted. Although Bowler said he would appeal to the court of the quarter sessions to have it quashed, he paid the penalty and Fox had not had a complaint about him since. Fox was not aware that Bowler had made any alteration to his factory in order to solve the problem but solve the problem he did.

Fox only had one case of a low chimney not being resolved. That belonged to John Osmond Lee, a baker at Chorlton-on-Ardwick, who believed he'd been prosecuted because he was a poor man. It was only after repeated complaints that Fox had summoned him before a magistrate. A gentleman who had an estate close by asked the baker to come to his premises and inhale his own smoke, but he refused. Lee appeared before a magistrate to argue the case but the decision went against him and he was given a penalty of forty shillings. Fox explained that if he received no more complaints, no further proceedings would be taken against him. He now used coke, and there had never been further complaint.

Fox told the committee that the aim of proceeding in this way had not been to convict the offenders but to prevent the offence from continuing.

Fox considered the issue of raising chimneys. He told the committee that in the majority of cases in which proceedings had been taken, the chimneys had been raised at minor expense because it required just a few yards of piping. Fox did not compel chimneys to be raised to the full height, provided they were raised to a sufficient height to reduce the nuisance and prevent complaints. Fox was not aware of any works where a chimney could not be raised.

The committee then turned to ways in which smoke was produced. There were a number of ironworks in Manchester, including one called Vickers, which was making smoke in the old-fashioned way. However, as they were preparing to construct modern works, Fox had not proceeded against them as he appreciated that they were taking steps to alter their manufacturing processes.

Fox said there were some very offensive chimneys in the dyeing trade and he thought they were probably all cotton goods. However, he had noticed that there were two chimneys, one belonging to a Mr Wainwright and one to a Mr Bignold, which did not emit such foul smoke as the others, even though all the smoke came from steam engines or furnaces. Fox did not know enough about the dyeing process to understand why or how these were producing less smoke but he knew that if they could do it, then so could everyone else.

He told the committee that he issued proceedings in two cases. One was if people in the neighbourhood complained to him and the other was when he observed the nuisance himself. If he received a complaint, no matter how large or influential the works, it would be if investigated and, if considered to be a nuisance, dealt with at once. If he saw a chimney smoking he would walk straight in to the building and tell the people that it wasn't allowed.

Fox had received complaints of smithy fires (which are heated in the open air) and other fires in connection with Galloway's, the boilermakers. Fox had frequent conversations with Galloway in reference to all his chimneys, which were said to be offensive to the neighbours. After a considerable amount of toing and froing, Fox succeeded in getting him to install five more chimneys 90ft high. Fox thought Galloway went to great inconvenience to make the alterations but it solved the problem and there was no further complaint about his works.

Fox told the committee that all the complaints in his area were remedied following his intervention. The businesses would make adjustments, the smoke would reduce and the neighbours would be happy.

Winsford 1893, Ralph Oakes

He had been in the shaft, cleared all the rubbish out and cleaned the salt rock head. He said no man in England could tell whether water was coming in or not.

Bill to provide compensation for owners of property suffering through the subsidence of the ground caused by the Brine Pumping (Compensation for Subsidence) Bill in 1893.

Winsford population growth

1801	981
1851	2,575
1901	16,382

Ralph Oakes was inspector of nuisances for one of the sanitary authorities of Winsford in Cheshire. He gave evidence in the House of Commons on the Brine Pumping (Compensation for Subsidence) Bill in 1893.

Shafts were sunk to get to the brine and rock salt, which were commercially valuable and used in a variety of manufacturing processes. Oakes was experienced in sinking shafts – he told the committee he had sunk more shafts than all the men in Cheshire. He was, he said, such an expert sinker that he had even sunk in foreign countries, such as Spain. The committee began by asking Oakes about some unusual matter that had been brought out of the abandoned number four shaft near Moulton Hill, New Bridge.

Oakes said he had never worked on that shaft but he had seen what had come out of it and he described it as glacial drift. He said that in all his time, he'd never seen this matter – which consisted of rocks and sediment – before.

Oakes told the committee that for years he had been saying there was a great fault running to a great depth between Bostock Green and New Bridge Salt Works. Oakes said he knew this as he had examined almost every well in the district and knew the area very well. He believed the fault was the cause of the glacial drift.

Oakes then turned his attention to the levels of brine in the area. He had been asked by the Salt Chamber of Commerce to take the levels of the brine at Winsford and surrounding areas. He did this for three months and found that there was much more brine at Winsford than there was at New Bridge. He believed that at New Bridge the river was about 30ft lower, so the salt rock head would be nearer to the surface at New Bridge than at Winsford, and this he believed was the reason for the difference in quantity of brine.

The committee asked Oakes if there had always been a shortage of brine at New Bridge. Oakes said yes but added that when he had been taking salt measurements, there was no shortage of brine at Northwich. Oakes also said that when there had been a large rainfall, the supply of brine increased.

However, the rainfall was bringing its problems as well. It had been claimed, by a witness who had contacted the committee the day before, that water from a shaft had got into the Bostock Green works. That witness was Jabez Anderson, who used to work as a foreman at Joseph Verdin & Sons' Newbridge Works. He said that water had come in and the hole had been plugged twice. Oakes said he did not believe that for a moment, for he had been in the shaft, cleared all the rubbish out and cleaned the salt rock head. He said no man in England could tell whether water was coming in or not.

The committee suggested that if that was the case, Oakes could not tell if water was coming in either. Oakes said he had the testimony of the banksman and the managers of the works that no such occurrence ever took place, and even though the committee added that a Mr Anderson, who was also employed at the works, had said water was present, Oakes continued to stick to his word.

Bradford 1910, James Swinburne

He thought it was possible to avoid emitting black smoke. Indeed, he thought manufacturers could avoid emitting dark smoke.

Bill to confer powers upon the Lord Mayor, aldermen and citizens of the city of Bradford for the construction of tramways and street works; to authorise the use of trolley vehicles; to alter the style and title of the Corporation and to make provisions with respect to various matters of local administration and management.

Bradford population growth

1801	6,000
1851	108,000
1901	279,000

James Swinburne was a highly experienced consulting engineer and a Fellow of the Royal Society. He gave evidence on the Bradford Corporation Bill in 1910 concerning the amount of smoke in Bradford. In recent years, he had been called repeatedly to advise on how to protect against smoke and how to minimize it. In his opinion Bradford had too much smoke and it was a nuisance that needed to be dealt with, but delicately.

Swinburne observed that the prevention of serious smoke was a small matter to the trader but a large matter to the public. He knew it was not possible to stop all smoke – no furnace could stop producing smoke completely – and he didn't think all smoke was harmful. Consequently, he was wary of passing this bill, which wanted to haul before the court anyone who was considered to be making too much smoke.

Sometimes he saw smoke coming out of the corporation's chimney, which supplied the electricity, and he didn't consider that to do any harm because it was vapour that had partly condensed and evaporated again. It also only lasted for about 20 to 30yrds, and then disappeared completely. Thus, he wasn't trying to stop all smoke, only that which he considered to be a nuisance.

Swinburne believed that as smoke was being reduced everywhere, and the processes behind manufacturing, furnace-working and methods of burning were improving, it might be possible to abolish smoke completely in the future. But not now. One could not create perfect furnaces by an Act of Parliament.

Swinburne, therefore, thought the words in the bill that said businesses should 'consume or burn the smoke' should not mean consume or burn *all* the smoke. The reason for that was because although whoever wrote the bill knew that factories used what was termed as 'smoke-consuming furnaces' these could only consume *most* not *all* of the smoke.

He certainly did not see why a question of very light smoke should be brought before a magistrate. He did not see any need for it. However, if this bill was passed, this is what would happen.

A magistrate would then have to consider two things. First, the extent of the nuisance or damage caused by the smoke, and the expense or inconvenience required to obviate that. He had to hold a fair hand between the two. In some cases he might think the damage done by the smoke, if any, was so small that the large expense was unreasonable. In others, he would say 'large though the expense is, the damage done was great.' All one could ask on behalf of the Bradford manufacturers was that the magistrates should have the power to deal with the cases on an individual basis and not with a single law. In the current set up, the magistrate had no other course except to inflict a fine, and Swinburne felt that a fine would not always be fair.

Despite this, Swinburne was an advocate for the reduction of smoke, and his objective was to half the amount currently leaving Bradford's chimneys. He thought it was certainly possible to avoid emitting black smoke. Indeed, he thought manufacturers could avoid emitting dark smoke.

He was happy to penalize the traders who sent out black smoke by using the furnaces negligently but didn't believe they should be punished if it was an accident. This was because businesses, such as Lister's, a large textile company in Bradford, were using the furnaces correctly but were working on how they could control the smoke and in doing so, a form of trial and error resulted in black smoke being produced on occasion.

Normally, the furnace would consume most of its own smoke. If any person used a furnace which wasn't constructed to consume or burn most of its own smoke, that would be an offence. However, the legislation left the whole question of fines, penalties and reasonableness to the magistrate. If the magistrate was reasonable, then the legislation seemed fair to Swinburne, but if the lawman came down too hard on the trader, it would be grossly unfair.

Woolwich 1910, James Court

He had noticed that the worst offenders were the factories belonging to the Crown.

Bill to empower the London County Council to execute street works and acquire lands, to confer other powers upon that Council and upon sanitary authorities in the administrative County of London; to provide for the licensing of employment agencies; to empower the Council of the Metropolitan Borough of Camberwell to acquire certain lands, and for other purposes.

Woolwich population growth

1801	9,826
1851	41,625
1901	41,625

James Court was Woolwich Council's inspector of nuisances and gave evidence before the House of Commons select committee on the London County Council (General Powers) Bill in 1910. He told the committee that from 1 January 1892 to 1 April 1909 he had been employed as a coal officer, and from 1879 to 1909 was engaged exclusively in the south-east district of London.

His duties during that period included making observations of smoke nuisance and, in the course of his work, he had noticed that the worst offenders were the factories belonging to the Crown. Court said he had appealed to Woolwich Borough Council for help as not only did he have difficulty in prosecuting these manufacturers but when he attempted to charge private manufacturers for causing similar problems, he was met with the response: 'We should not be prosecuted when the greater offenders, namely the Government's factories, are not dealt with.'

Currently, the amount of smoke generated by the Government's chimneys was so great that it was occupying virtually all Court's time.

Only the week before, Court had observed, made notes on and taken pictures of the Arsenal chimneys on three separate days. On the first day, number five shaft emitted smoke for fifty minutes over a three-hour period; a short circular shaft was smoking for eighteen minutes; number one shaft was smoking for ten minutes, and other shafts were smoking for twenty-five, forty-four and thirty-three minutes respectively.

Court believed that if this amount of smoke had been caused by a private manufacturer, proceedings would have been taken. Indeed, Court told the committee that private traders had been penalized for producing far less smoke.

These were not one-offs. The factories worked like this every day because they knew they were protected by virtue of belonging to the Crown. On day three of his observations, he saw shaft number five smoking for forty-four minutes; another shaft for thirty minutes; another for sixteen; another for fifteen and another for fourteen minutes. It was a constant problem and the very worst type of pitch black smoke.

Court then produced photographs illustrating what he had seen. The committee asked whether these chimneys were all being worked at the same time, and he replied that in some cases they were and in other cases they were operating singularly. The committee observed that, of the group of chimneys pictured, only some were emitting black smoke. Court said that was because the others were not in use.

Court reiterated that this wasn't fair and if he had pictorial proof of private chimneys smoking in that way, proceedings would have been taken against them.

Chapter 14

Burial Grounds

Great Northern London Cemetery 1855, Alfred Taylor

*Having cemeteries that weren't fit for purpose gave rise to
the disgusting practice in London of burning the remains of
the dead.*

Bill for making and maintaining the Great Northern London Cemetery,
and for other purposes.

With London's population growing at an alarming rate, a number of new
cemeteries had been built in the mid-nineteenth century and in 1855, the
large Great Northern London Cemetery was proposed on a site at Brunswick
Park Road in the borough of Barnet. It is now known as New Southgate
Cemetery. The Great Northern London Cemetery Company had been set
up to run the cemetery that would consist of 145 acres. Cemeteries were
an important part of society and were visited regularly. London cemeteries
even had their own railway stations. The Great Northern London Cemetery
Company was aiming at the lower end of the market. It proposed to charge
six shillings to carry a coffin, plus a return train fare of one shilling and
sixpence for each mourner, plus a burial fee starting at ten or eleven shillings.

Dr Alfred S. Taylor was a Government consultant on nuisances in
London and had been consulted by the Home Office regarding nuisances
in cemeteries. He had, therefore, been asked to visit the site to assess
its suitability and had found the land was mainly a clay soil, which was
known as London clay. Taylor had been called in as a perfectly impartial
person and had inspected the proposed site the day before he gave
evidence in Parliament and spent six-and-a-half hours there.

The committee on the Northern London Cemetery Bill 1855 had
already heard some evidence and knew it was a gravelly soil. Taylor had

found it was not strictly gravel and the soil was about 5ft 10ins in depth but only 4ft of this was dry as then it was filled with water.

The site had been divided into pits and in one, chosen at random, Taylor had found 1ft 10ins of it was filled with water. Clay mixed with pebbles would be permeable by water and he found pebbles of different sizes cemented by clay, with seams of clay round the side. However, this only went so far down because, after prodding the soil with a stick, Taylor discovered that below the water was plastic clay. The water covered the whole of the lower part, so he could not see where the pebbles stopped. The water must have been standing there for some time because there had been no rain for several weeks and there was an impermeable stratum on which it was resting. It was the stratum in which all the shallow wells and pumps of London were sunk, and this was what made London a bad place for burial.

Next, Taylor examined two other pits: numbers seventeen and twenty-one. Those were described as 'opponents' pits'. There was no appearance of gravel about them, but they were filled up with London clay.

Pit number five was near the top of the hill and looked like a roughly made grave. Taylor found water in it. The pit was 8ft long and 4ft wide. Its sides were formed of large loosely rolled pebbles with seams of clay and the whole of one side had fallen in. The depth in the centre was 6ft 10ins of which 2ft 4ins was water and 4ft 6ins consisted of pebbles with seams of clay. There was 28ins of water. This satisfied Taylor that there was no natural drainage.

If graves were dug on this site, there would be no natural drainage unless the bodies were placed within 2ft of the surface, which would not be appropriate. When burying the dead, the objective is for the bodies to decompose as quickly as possible without any injury to the living. If the grave is very deep, the air temperature does not affect the body and it remains unchanged for a long time and decomposition is severely delayed. However, Taylor thought nobody should be buried any less than 5 or 6ft deep in order to avoid the effect of the cracks and the porous nature of the soil permitting the exhalations to escape. Judging from the appearance of that stratum, Taylor believed that less than 6ft would hardly be desirable.

Unless the bodies had been buried very deep, in hot weather the large fissures, which could be observed in the clay, let out noxious gases. And there was no chance of the sun drying the water out as it would be constantly recurring. He said the test of a good graveyard was a very simple one: that a person should be able to dig down 8ft, allow that pit to be opened for a month and that there should be no collection of water. This was not the cause in any of the pits he was examining.

The company's pit, also at the top of the hill, was one of the deepest. It was 8ft 6ins and no less than 4ft 6ins had water in it. There was 4ft of pebbly clay and Taylor calculated that it contained 600 gallons of water. Another pit – number four – which also belonged to the company, was filled up entirely and Taylor could not see the bottom of it. Number three pit was on the hill. It was 5ft 10ins deep with 2ft of water and only 3ft 10ins of dry soil.

The level of the water in the pits was much higher than that in a nearby brook's, although after examination he concluded that it was not coming from the brook, which was about 10yrds away. Unfortunately, the only place the water from the graves could drain into was the brook, which ran between two slopes. He said it was intolerable that a large cemetery that was likely to last for centuries, should be allowed to drain into that brook and then the River Lea. He could not believe that anyone should be allowed to put coffins in water to allow them to putrefy, and then let the water from that flow into the environment. He conceded that certain amounts of effluvium dissolved or was converted by natural processes into other shapes, but added that this would not happen with the amount of bodies buried here.

He added that in London, water drawn from pumps near graveyards often contained organic matter. The only way to avoid this was to not build a cemetery on London clay. He said it was a complete disregard of everything that had been recommended in the evidence before the Board of Health and that was not only the consensus in England but also on the continent. He had seen burials in Naples and in Paris, and in other parts, and the general view was London clay was the worst possible soil for this use.

He explained that if a dead body was placed in a loose porous soil – a mixture of sand and gravel with a little mould – any rainwater would pass through the grave and not macerate the body. If any moisture did affect the body, the moderate access to air would mean the body would gradually decompose and gradually give off gases. The process would be so slow that Taylor did not think any material effluvium would arise, and in eight to twelve years the whole of the body would have disappeared.

If buried in London clay, the water would sit at the bottom of the grave and keep the body moist. This would alter the course of putrefaction and the body would slowly become converted into a fatty, waxy compound called adipocere or 'grave wax'. Taylor knew this for a fact. In the course of his role, he had examined a great number of bodies at all periods of interment, from one month to four years after burial, and he had seen how damp graves produced adipocere. All the soft parts were converted into a waxy compound and stayed liked that for fifteen to twenty years.

Another side effect of London clay was that insects attacked it. Taylor had to disinter a body just a year before and, on removing the lid of the coffin, the shroud and a part of the body were covered with insects. The insects had eaten some, but not all of the body. The rest had been converted to adipocere. In order to prove his point, Taylor had the remains of a body, which had been buried on 22 December 1852, dug up the May before the committee hearing in 1855. As predicted, it was in a state of adipocere and the body was not entirely decomposed.

There was a churchyard riddled with water in Hampstead Road, which had not, for some reason, been shut down despite the fact that when any grave was dug, 3 or 4ft of water came into it. Taylor said a relative of his had been buried in the graveyard and the ground was so wet that after a few years, he had found it quite impossible to trace the grave. It also meant that when the ground was opened near to the place of a recent interment in order to bury a body, the foul air and putrid water that had entered into the grave from the side produced such a stink that the gravedigger was obliged to leave it for a time before interment could take place. This caused an unwelcome delay for the bereaved.

Having cemeteries that weren't fit for purpose gave rise to the disgusting practice in London of burning the remains of the dead. This was so prevalent that specially made flues or chimneys were built for the sole purpose of burning the bodies and getting rid of everything altogether – coffin, wood and remains.

Taylor believed the only way of solving the issue was to drain the land on which these cemeteries had been built, thoroughly and deeply. However, he also knew that if drainage took place from every grave, it would be carried away into the neighbourhood. And this would be a lot of water – he had seen 600 gallons in one grave alone. He did not see how such a quantity of contaminated water could be got rid of over a large area without damaging the health of the people around it. It wasn't possible to drain the ground once and for all and leave it as the water was constantly flowing through.

He calculated that from about 6,000 bodies buried annually, there would be about a ton of animal matter left. With regards to the bodies themselves, Taylor had done some experiments to determine the actual weight of the bones as well as the soft parts and other sections to ascertain what would be the result and he presented the committee with his findings.

The dead body of an adult male weighed around 150lbs. One hundred parts would be thus constituted: dry bones 6lbs; dry matter and soft matter from the muscles 18lbs; water 75lbs. The only solid matter left in the grave would be some 4 to 5lbs. The other parts would be resolved into gases or into liquids.

Assuming the 6,000 bodies were buried at the level of where the water was, the liquid would be fetid, consisting of decomposed blood, decomposed muscle, decomposed brain and, in fact, all the soft organs of the body. The rest would have been absorbed or imbibed by the clay. But, Taylor added, one of the great evils of graveyards in clay was that clay was a very absorbent substance and it absorbed those foul liquids. When a fresh grave was dug and turned over, the exposure of that to the air and the heat of the sun led to the evolution of very noxious effluvia.

Taylor showed the committee the internal organs of a woman who had died two-and-a-half years before. He produced them quickly to give a notion of the seriousness of the stench it produced. He said that if it were laid out in a space twice the size of the committee room, it would clear the room in about five minutes.

He was worried there would be difficulty in proving the direct effect of effluvia upon health although he was convinced that it was very bad. Since the previous October, on orders of the Secretary of State and the police commissioners, Taylor had inspected over 200 factories evolving offensive chemical effluvia. He had been to bone-boiling establishments of Lambeth, cat-gut manufacturers, glue manufacturers and other places that could give rise to effluvium. However, in every establishment, he was assured that they all had excellent health, never a day's illness, and that the cholera had not appeared around that spot at all.

Despite this, Taylor believed the effluvium damaged the whole health of London by getting into the atmosphere. If it did not poison the population directly in the event of an epidemic, it put their bodies in a lesser capacity to resist the effects of disease. The mortality in London was greater than that in the country, although he conceded that there were many things beside graveyards that might be the cause. Taylor did not know if there was a greater mortality in the neighbourhoods around the cemeteries but added that the necessary effects of effluvia were not confined to a few yards.

Taylor was asked about other London cemeteries that had been completed within the past two years, principally St Pancras, Finchley, Kensal Green and Marylebone cemeteries. He believed Finchley had the most favourable soil as it was not all London clay but a mixture of surface clay and gravel. Taylor had not been consulted about Finchley Cemetery.

Taylor knew that for a parochial burial ground to be built, one must have the consent of the Secretary of State. St Pancras was a parochial burial ground, as was Marylebone but the Secretary of State had not consulted Taylor about these two burial grounds either. Taylor was not acquainted with the drainage arrangements of the new cemeteries around London. He knew that Kensal Green Cemetery was built on London clay but again, as he had not been consulted on it, he didn't know whether it drained into the Grand Junction Canal. If it did, it would flow into water that was still – except when it might be moved by boats passing along – and he thought this would be most improper. At Kensal Green, Taylor saw water in a grave which was 3ft from the surface. He said if the Government had asked his opinion, he would have said it was not a suitable place for interments.

He thought it unbelievable that the cemeteries of the metropolis were not acquainted with the sanitary considerations heeded abroad, where it was customary to choose the most suitable soils for burial and build cemeteries only on such soil. Of the eight cemeteries in London, five consisted of soil either wholly or in great part composed of clay which was perhaps the worst of all kinds of ground for interments. It was a recognized fact that different soils facilitated or retarded the process of decomposition and loose, open, porous ground was generally selected, but such a choice was utterly impractical in London.

The committee asked Taylor if it was desirable for a cemetery to select a spot as far from gentlemen's residences as possible. Taylor's view was that it was desirable to keep a good space between them. He said he would certainly object to living in a house close enough to a graveyard that the water could be drained into the ornamental water feature in his garden. Not only could it endanger his and his family's health but the smell would be appalling. He had no doubt that the further from London and populated areas, the better the site would be. Taylor's ideal was being further from London with the additional advantage of there being a better soil there – a porous soil. He identified Woking Common as a perfect location. Additionally, the soil on the south of the river was considerably better adapted for the purpose of sepulchres than any to the north. He added that where there was a lot of sandy soil, the body was soon converted into a mummy.

Taylor concluded by telling the committee he knew enough about the land on which the Great Northern London Cemetery was proposed to be built and he would attempt to dissuade the Government from using it for such a purpose. It was Taylor's most candid opinion that no site could be worse selected for the burial of the dead.

Conclusion

Britain's population rose from 8,893,000 to 33,526,000 in the nineteenth century and this put a great strain on a society that had little running water, no mains sewerage and few flush toilets. This rudimentary sanitation resulted in all sorts of 'nuisances' from a lack of water, shrimps in the drinking water, dead dogs floating in the streets, streams full of human waste and waterlogged graves.

Life expectancy during the nineteenth century rose from around 40 to 50, while an expanding industry covered the towns and cities with a layer of soot and grime, and were largely indifferent to the consequences for public health. Row upon row of terraced housing, built on either side of a railway track with a locomotive engine in full steam on it, sprung up in our urban areas. Small children left their overcrowded homes to run alongside the tracks while the constant plumes of smoke dirtied their clothes and clogged up their lungs.

Coal consumption during the nineteenth century rose from 10 million tons in 1800 to 250 million tons a century later. In contrast, coal consumption had fallen to 31 million tons by the year 2000, with obvious benefits to the environment and people.

The newly established local authorities of 1835 cut their teeth on dealing with the consequent filth of daily life. This they did partly through an army of inspectors of nuisances, whose work covered many aspects of modern-day local government. These inspectors contributed greatly to the health and safety of Britain's Victorian cities, and to the lengthening of life expectancy. Life at the end of the century was less grimy, more hygienic, healthier and safer thanks in no small part to their work. People were living longer in a cleaner domestic environment. Life was not so nasty, brutish and short as it had been in 1900.

Nuisance inspectors are now a thing of the past. The last evidence session in Parliament to feature an inspector was during the

Conclusion

First World War. Most of the grime that coated Britain's great Victorian industrial cities has now been cleaned away, although this took many decades. The Great Smog of London in 1952, was said to have killed around 4,000 people with many more becoming ill from its effects. The change in industry and manufacturing means that smoking mill chimneys no longer dominate the skyline of Bradford; no blackened town halls stand proudly in northern cities and towns.

Today the inspectors of nuisances have been replaced by a range of local authority officers who address problems of food hygiene, trading standards, health and safety, anti-social behaviour, environmental health and the safety of buildings. The country is a better place for their work and that of their predecessors.

Appendix 1

National Population Growth

National population growth 1801 to 1901		
Year	Total	Increase
1801	8,893,000	–
1811	10,164,000	1,271,000
1821	12,000,000	1,836,000
1831	13,897,000	1,897,000
1841	15,914,000	2,017,000
1851	17,928,000	2,014,000
1861	20,066,000	2,138,000
1871	22,712,000	2,646,000
1881	25,974,000	3,262,000
1891	29,003,000	3,029,000
1901	33,526,000	4,523,000

Appendix 2

Occupations of the Witnesses

Numbers in brackets indicate the number of sessions which featured a man of that occupation:-

Architect, surveyor and estate agent
Chairman of pleasure boat committee
Clergyman (2)
Government consultant on nuisances
Inspector of nuisances (36)
Inspector of nuisances, architect
Inspector of nuisances, borough meat inspector
Inspector of nuisances, chief (4)
Inspector of nuisances, chief sanitary inspector
Inspector of nuisances, superintendent of police
Inspector of nuisances, surveyor (2)
Officer in charge of nuisances
Sanitary inspector
Superintendent cleansing and watering

Appendix 3

Locations to Which the Evidence Sessions Relate

Numbers in brackets indicate more than one evidence session relating to that place:-

Beverley
Birmingham (4)
Blackburn
Bolton
Bradford (3)
Bradford, Eccleshill
Bridlington
Bristol
Bury
Caerphilly
Cardiff
Cheltenham
Chepstow
Clapton
Consett and Knitsley
Darwen
Great Yarmouth
Guildford
Halifax
Hartlepool
Horfield
Hyde
Ilford
Leeds

Locations to Which the Evidence Sessions Relate

Leicester (2)
Lincoln
Liverpool (3)
London (5)
Acton
East Ham (2)
Great Northern London Cemetery
Woolwich
Manchester
Meriden
Mynyddislwyn
Norwich
Pudsey
Rawmarsh
Rock Ferry
Rotherham
Runcorn
Skegness
Thirsk
Whitehaven
Winsford
Wolverhampton
Yeovil

Index

Acts of Parliament
Leeds Improvement Act 1856 78, 79
Municipal Corporations Act 1835
 x, 2, 83
Nuisances Removal and Diseases
 Prevention Act 1846 xi, 2, 6,
 8, 30
Public Health Act 1890 22, 23,
 34, 67
Rivers Pollution Prevention Act
 1876 66

Abercarn 92
Acton (W London) 22-23
Adipocere ('grave wax') 104
Armitage, William 80-81
Ash pits 11, 18, 54, 58, 59, 60
Aylesford, Lord 43

Banks, Joseph 13-16, 69-72
Bazalgette, Joseph 3
Beverley 4, 59-60
Billingsgate Fish Market 70
Birmingham ix, 3, 8-9, 75-77
Birth rate ix
Blackburn 81-83
Bland, William 56-57
Blenheim Palace 4
Bliss, James 3, 75-77

Bolton 56-57
Bookmakers, nuisance caused by
 14-15
Booth, William 29-31
Bradbury, John xi
Bradford ix, xi, 6-7, 29, 30, 54,
 55, 73-74, 97-99
Bretherton, Samuel 42-44
Bridlington 12-13
Brine pumping, nuisance caused
 by 96-97
Bristol 55-56; Water Company
 20, 21
Brooks, Joseph 35-36
Brown, George 26-27
Brown, James xi, 91-92
Bure, River 64, 67
Burial grounds see Cemeteries
Bury 85-88
Butchers see Slaughterhouses
Bute, Marquis of 62, 63

Caerphilly 44-46
Caldicot 41
Cardiff 62-64; Bute Docks 62
Castle Howard 4
Catton (Norwich) 35
Cemeteries, problems with
 drainage of 18, 51, 101ff;

Severn Tunnel, effect on local
    water supplies 41
Sewage farms 50
Shustoke 43
Slaughterhouses and butchers,
    nuisance caused by 24, 50, 52,
    72, 75ff, 85
Smallpox 89
Smith, John 49-51
Smog, in London, 1952 109
Smoke and chimneys, nuisance
    cause by 93-95, 98-99, 100
Sowerby 17, 19
Sprowston (Norwich) 35
Stockton & Darlington
    Railway 40
Swale, William 78-80
Swinburne, James 97-99

Taff, River 62, 63
Taylor, Dr Alfred S. xi, 101
Thirsk 17-19
Thompson, George 38-40
Throston (Hartlepool) 61
Tottington (Lancs) 87
Town, Joseph 53-55
Travellers 13-16
Treorchy 63
Tyersal (Bradford) 54

Tyldesley, William xi, 72-73
Typhus/typhoid fever 26, 87

Undercliffe 30-31
Upton-on-Severn 53

Vickers, John Smiles 4, 59-60

Waterworks companies 11, 21,
    28, 31, 32, 36, 56, 84
Wells and springs 10, 18, 19, 20,
    27, 33, 39, 49, 56, 85
West Ham 16
Whiston 11
White, Charles 19-22
White, Frank xi, 73-74
Whitehaven 49-51
Wholesalers, prosecution of for
    selling unfit food 70-72, 73
Williams, Rev William 40-42
Williams, Robert 48
Williams, Thomas 62-64
Winsford 95-97
Wolverhampton 27-29
Woolwich 99-100
Wright, John 17-19
Wroxham 66

Yeovil 48-49